GROWING UP GREEN

Education
for
Ecological Renewal

GROWING UP GREEN

Education for Ecological Renewal

David Hutchison

FOREWORD by Thomas Berry

Teachers College, Columbia University
New York and London

R

Published by Teachers College Press, 1234 Amsterdam Avenue, New York, NY 10027

Copyright © 1998 by Teachers College, Columbia University

Selected extracts in Chapter 4 are from *The Ecology of Imagination in Childhood* by Edith Cobb. Copyright © 1977 by Columbia University Press. Reprinted with permission of the publisher.

Library of Congress Cataloging-in-Publication Data

Hutchison, David C.
    Growing up green : education for ecological renewal / David
Hutchison.
        p.   cm.
    Includes bibliographical references and index.
    ISBN 0-8077-3725-9 (cloth). — ISBN 0-8077-3724-0 (paper)
    1. Environmental education — Philosophy.   2. Green movement.
I. Title.
GE70.H8   1998
363.7′0071′2 — dc21   97-43995

ISBN 0-8077-3724-0 (paper)
ISBN 0-8077-3725-9 (cloth)

Printed on acid-free paper
Manufactured in the United States of America

05 04 03 02 01 00 99 98   8 7 6 5 4 3 2 1

To my parents,
and
in memory of
Paul Shepard
1925–1996

Beneath the veneer of civilization . . . lies not the barbarian and animal, but the human in us who knows the rightness of birth in gentle surroundings, the necessity of a rich nonhuman environment, play at being animals, the discipline of natural history, juvenile tasks with simple tools, the expressive arts of receiving food as a spiritual gift rather than as a product, the cultivation of metaphorical significance of natural phenomena of all kinds, clan membership and small-group life, and the profound claims and liberation of ritual initiation and subsequent stages of adult mentorship. There is a secret person undamaged in every individual, aware of the validity of these, sensitive to their right moments in our lives. All of them are assimilated in perverted forms in modern society: our profound love of animals twisted into pets, zoos, decorations, and entertainment; our search for poetic wholeness subverted by the model of the machine instead of the body; the moment of pubertal idealism shunted into nationalism or ethereal otherworldly religion instead of an ecosophical cosmology. But this means that we have not lost, and cannot lose, the genuine impulse. It awaits only an authentic expression. The task is not to start by recapturing the theme of a reconciliation with the earth in all of its metaphysical subtlety, but with something much more direct and simple that will yield its own healing metaphysics.

—Paul Shepard, *Nature and Madness* (1982)

The six-year-old [is] confronted with the cosmic plan. The universe [is] presented to the child's imagination.

—Maria Montessori, *To Educate the Human Potential* (1948/1967)

Contents

Acknowledgments

A number of people played key roles in supporting me throughout the preparation of this book. Professor David Selby of the Institute for Global Education, University of Toronto, supervised the writing of the initial draft of the manuscript and made a number of key suggestions for improvement. I am also indebted to Professor Leesa Fawcitt of the Faculty of Environmental Studies, York University, who supervised my early research. I would also like to thank Professor Edmund Sullivan, of the Ontario Institute for Studies in Education, who encouraged me to link my educational reform proposals to the cosmological insights of Thomas Berry. I am also indebted to Thomas Berry, who agreed to write the Foreword.

This book is a product of several years of reflection and practical experience working with children. I wish to thank Jim Baker, of the School for Experiential Education, who helped me to frame my initial interest in education. I am also indebted to Professor Deborah Berrill, of the Faculty of Education, Queen's University, who encouraged me as I struggled to articulate my emerging philosophy of education during my undergraduate years. During these same years, Professors Robert Carter and Lionel Rubinoff supervised my formal study of the philosophy of education at Trent University.

I am also indebted to my parents, without whose support this book would not have been possible. This book is dedicated to them.

Foreword

The twentieth century has been one of strange contrasts. We have learned a great deal about the universe, yet we have also lost our intimacy with it. The skills we have invented for our grand space adventures are the same ones that enable us to despoil the air, soil, and waters of their life-giving powers. As our artificial transformation of nature advances, our presence to nature declines. We live in a plundering industrial world of wires, wheels, and machines, of steel and plastics, of paved-over land and poisoned seas.

Earlier peoples lived amid the stars. Human affairs were coordinated with the movement of the heavens and the sequence of the seasons, with dawn and sunset, with the comings and goings of the animals in their migratory journeys. Today we live amid the turmoil and anxiety of a world that we have made ourselves and which we must sustain in existence and care for out of our own powers. We toil endlessly to produce, market, and care for the artificial world, the constantly disintegrating environment we have created.

In the earlier, pre-industrial period, demands were made on humans, yet the benefits were also there for the taking. Imagination and emotions were filled with the mystery and wonder of forests, deserts, and coastal lands. The universe ran on an intimacy of everything with everything. It was a world of persons and powers, of beauty and mystery, of wonder and poetry—albeit with an ever-present threat to life and survival, the harshness of the seasons, the loss of children, the constant need to hunt and gather food. Life was precarious in the extreme. It was a threatening world as well as a sustaining one.

Yet there was, with the invention of gardening and pasturing, a way of mitigating the uncertainties of life, while continuing the intimacy with its powers. There was also an attrition on the land. Humans evidently contributed to the decline and extinction of the megaform animals. Even so, there was on the whole a viable way of life that sustained the comprehensive order of things. This sense of belonging and of being cared for found expression in the Omaha Indian ritual of announcing the birth of a newborn child to the universe and commending the child to the powers of the heavens; to the wind, the rain, the forests and woodland creatures, and even to the insects and those living forms that reside within the earth.

All these phenomena were recognized in an intimate, caring relation to the child. Nothing existed alone in this world. The great Covenant of the Universe, the intimacy of each mode of being with all other modes of being, was instilled by genetic coding into each component of the living world. With the human, however, there was the necessity of a conscious bonding with the other components of the universe. This is the origin of schooling, especially in the middle years of childhood between six and twelve. The primary purpose of those years was not only to bring the child into its adult role in society; it was also to bring the child and the universe into an intimacy with each other through ritual and song and especially the narratives of society.

If language is learned in the earlier years, it is the language of the universe as well as human language. Little children especially love to imitate the voices of animals, the wind, and all other natural phenomena. So now in these middle years, this intimacy is more profoundly developed; for the child discovers both her personal self in the unique features of her own body, in her own thought and emotions, in her own talents, in her own sensitivities. Yet she also needs to experience her personal self in relation to her greater self; her social self, and most important, her universe self.

Maria Montessori recognized that for the six-year-old child there is a special need for a bonding with the universe. In her view, the universe was "the answer to all questions." Awareness of this comprehensive world of meaning awakens in the child both a sense of grandeur and a sense of responsibility. It stirs the imagination to poetry and the arts and thus leads to profound imaginative as well as emotional fulfillment. We might say that the universe and the child are fulfilled in each other. It takes a universe to bring a child into being. It takes a universe to educate a child. It takes a universe to fulfill a child. While this could be said, in some manner, of every being in the universe, it has special application to the human child, who needs to go through an extensive period of conscious development beyond that needed for any other species of child that we know of.

It is the basic aim of this book to indicate that we have a remarkable opportunity to establish an integral education for children in their middle years and to recover, both for them and for ourselves, an integral mode of being in the great world of the living. Here in the formative years of youth we find the emotional and imaginative, as well as the intellectual, aptitude for resituating the human within a viable context for survival and for that level of entrancing fulfillment in the wonders of the universe that are so necessary for the human mode of being.

Thomas Berry
Greensboro, North Carolina

The Recovery of the Earth Process

*We are returning to our native place after a long absence, meeting once again
with our kin . . . as we recover our presence within the earth community.*
— Thomas Berry, *The Dream of the Earth*

This book explores the relationship of environmental advocacy to the philosophy of education and holistic theories of child development. It is argued
that the current public debate concerning the future of education, with its
largely limited focus on the school as a site of economic renewal, ignores a
much more substantive problem related to the deepening environmental
impasse and the role of the human in disrupting the ecological stability of
the planet. It is because the environmental problems we presently face are
so intricately related to the long-term future of our industrial economies
that we urgently need to address the challenges faced by the wider earth
community as we consider the future role to be played by schools in society.
Yet public debate on the topic of education and other social issues has
typically failed to acknowledge environmental problems as a pressing issue
of concern. Hence a true measure of our future economic and cultural
potential remains out of reach, skewed as it is by the fact that the prospects
for environmental recovery are not taken into full account.

Although the failure to address the needs of the wider earth community
is a significant omission on the part of educational commentators, the current debate on the "economics of education" nevertheless demonstrates
some striking parallels to the marginalized arguments of environmental
proponents. Advocates of both positions, for example, lay claim to having
developed a clear picture of what the future holds for coming generations.
Recognizing that schools have a special obligation to prepare young people
for the challenges that they will face as adults, each view forwards its own
(albeit divergent) vision for the future. The economic view is concerned
largely with looming economic problems, eased by the promise of economic
restructuring and the dawn of a postindustrial age; the environmental view

with looming environmental problems, eased by the promise of cultural and ecological renewal. Moreover, each view maintains that schools should play an active role in responding to these respective challenges. Rather than simply preserving those living traditions which have reproduced the same economic and environmental conditions of the past, schools are judged by proponents of both views to play an integral role in ushering in the promise of a new future age.

Implicit to the proposals of both economists and environmentalists is a recognition that schools throughout recent history have been charged with the task of formally instilling in each new generation, the norms and values of the existing culture. Even insofar as this role is now judged by some to be limited solely to training students in basic and job-related skills, schools nevertheless continue to play a key role in explicitly (and implicitly) orienting children to the basic values and modes of conduct of society. In recent years, much attention has been paid to other cultural influences on child socialization—for example, the role played by popular culture and television. Yet despite the often permeating influences of these important cultural factors, schools continue to be featured prominently in a vast majority of proposals for cultural and economic renewal—a tribute, perhaps, to both their enduring formal structure and their traditional role in providing a corrective or compensatory measure to children's education which serves to offset the unchecked influence of other decentralized or less formal institutions.

Given this view of schools, one would expect that the relationship between education and ideology might well represent a fertile ground of inquiry for environmental proponents who are deeply concerned about the enculturating role played by schools (and other institutions) in reproducing ecologically problematic values, attitudes, and behaviors across generations. Unfortunately, the evidence to date does not bear this out, for although the literature base on environmental education as a curricular area of study has grown considerably during the last several years, there are still relatively few publications which address the ideological relationship of education to the cultural dimensions of the environmental challenge. Most notable in this regard is the work of C. A. Bowers (1993), Gregory A. Smith (1992), and David W. Orr (1992). Bowers has sought, in part, to provide a detailed critique of the ecologically problematic elements of conservative, pragmatic, and emancipatory philosophies of education, while Smith has widened the critique to include the problematic aspects of modernism and industrialism as a whole. The chapters which follow echo a number of Orr's proposals for ecological literacy in schools and integrate selected aspects of the ideological critiques forwarded by Bowers and Smith, but also move beyond the critique mode to argue for a strengthening of the

relationship between environmental philosophies of education and ecologically sensitive theories of child development.

The last two decades have seen a quiet revolution in the research area
of holistic and ecologically sensitive developmental theory. Inspired in part
by the writings of Edith Cobb (1977), Harold F. Searles (1960), and Rachel
Carson (1956/1990) and the early research efforts of Roger Hart (1979), a
growing number of holistic researchers, including Thomas Armstrong
(1985), Robin C. Moore (1986), Joseph Chilton Pearce (1992), David Sobel (1993), and Gary Paul Nabhan and Stephen Trimble (1994) have
sought to delineate a developmental view of childhood which addresses the
important role played by peak experiences, story, place, and first-hand
contact with the natural world in promoting healthy development into
adulthood. To date, the significance of these explorations to education has
remained largely unaddressed. Yet such interpretative views of childhood
may be key to the development of a coherent and sustainable environmental
philosophy of education. Moreover, they may even point the way to a
renewed alliance between educational philosophy and the insights of developmental theory, an alliance originally forged almost a century ago by the
promise of progressive reform, but largely overshadowed in recent years by
the restricted notions of teaching as technique and schools as sites of economic renewal.

Chapter 1 explores the biological and cultural underpinnings of the
environmental challenge in terms of crises in ecology, economics, and consciousness. This chapter establishes the basis for understanding the ecologically problematic aspects of contemporary educational philosophy in the
next chapter. The emphasis is on the choices that we face as a society (and
as a species) in responding to this impasse. It is argued that during the
modern era we have gradually eroded the life systems and ecological processes of the planet to such a degree that our present ways of living are no
longer viable. Two separate courses of action seem to present themselves at
such a critical moment. To choose a Technozoic path is to place our faith
in the infinite ability of technology to get us out of the current crisis without
any need for us to change our consumptive lifestyles or relationship to
nature in any significant way. To choose an Ecozoic path is to forge a new
relationship with nature and the planet as a whole, first, by recognizing that
we are an interdependent part of the natural world, and second, by curbing
our destructive impact on the biological systems of the planet. This chapter
concludes that the Ecozoic path offers the only viable alternative if we are
to ensure the long-term future of the earth community.

Chapter 1 closes with the suggestion that most areas of cultural and
institutional life will likely face ecological redefinitions as the environmental
impasse grows more acute. Discussion in Chapter 2 applies this view to the

educational realm. Working from an environmental vantage point, this chapter reviews and critiques three contemporary philosophies of education, two which dominate the public discourse on educational practice, and a third which offers an alternative vision for education. A central question is which one of the three philosophies—technocratic, progressive, or holistic—forwards the most viable program of reform in light of the environmental challenges we presently face. An analysis of the ideological elements of each finds weaknesses in all three, but it is the holistic philosophy which seems to hold the most promise (at least at the ideological level), since neither the technocratic position nor the progressive position adequately addresses the fragile state of the planet's life systems or the role of the human within the larger context of the earth community. This chapter closes by considering briefly how potentially valuable practical elements from all three philosophies can find expression within a renewed vision of education.

Chapter 3 shifts the focus to an exploration of the cultural construction of childhood. This chapter provides the conceptual basis and launching point for a new story of early development that addresses the child's search for a functional cosmology of the universe during middle childhood. In attempting to account for variations in historical and cross-cultural constructions of childhood, this chapter outlines a cosmological model of childhood and explores the mythic foundations of selected traditions within contemporary developmental psychology. The concept of *functionality* is introduced as a way of assessing the effectiveness of specific constructions of childhood in meeting a young person's physical and psychosocial needs and further indicating the role and place of the child in the recovery of sustainable relations with the natural world.

Working within the constructivist perspective just established, Chapter 4 reviews a series of ecological and holistic models of development in middle childhood. It is argued that between the ages of about six and twelve, the child co-constructs a "working theory" of the universe built on a search for meaningfulness and purpose in the world of nature and the surrounding social and cultural worlds. An integrative discussion of several holistic conceptions of childhood, including those proposed by Friedrich Froebel, Maria Montessori, Rudolf Steiner, Edith Cobb, and Paul Shepard, establishes the basis for a new story of development in middle childhood and sets the stage for an overview of an ecologically sensitive approach to elementary education in the final chapter.

Chapter 4 closes with the criticism that both mainstream and holistic developmental theory have typically failed to account for the effects a loss of trust and security will have on development in childhood. In recognizing the likelihood that the environmental impasse we are now facing may soon strain many of the social supports afforded to children and families, Chapter 5 addresses this concern in relation to two examples of dysfunctionality in the cultural construction of childhood and by exploring the impact of community violence on children. In attempting to articulate the basic elements of a functional conception of childhood, the notion of childhood as a distinct ontological stage within the human life span is emphasized, as is the need for adults to play a supportive caregiving role in the lives of children. This chapter closes by considering briefly the impact environmental degradation and a declining resource base are now having on developing countries and may soon have on the lives of U.S. and Canadian children.

Chapter 6 outlines a methodology and curriculum for an ecologically sensitive approach to education in middle childhood, emphasizing the child's search for a working theory of the universe and other developmental insights from Chapter 4. An ecologically sensitive approach to education incorporates not only a spatial view of the universe rooted within the study of place and nature, but also a temporal vision of the unfolding of the universe through time. Hence there is a strong narrative quality to education during these years. Chapter 6 explores the role of nature study and gardening in elementary education, and the child's search for meaningfulness and purpose through the study of form. This chapter closes by considering what an ecologically sensitive approach to education in adolescence might entail.

In articulating an interdisciplinary position on environmental advocacy, the philosophy of education, and holistic theories of child development, this book is necessarily a formative and tentative view of an ecologically sensitive vision of childhood and education. I have no doubt that many of the themes and ideas which are explored will require further elaboration and more in-depth study. For myself and for those educators and readers who find these ideas to be of significance and worth pursuing, the years to come are certain to include much fruitful inquiry and collaboration among like-minded people who share a mutual concern for the future of the earth community and our responsibility to children. For these readers and others, I hope this book can serve as an invitation to further investigation and growth.

The Status of the Earth and of the Human at the Close of the Twentieth Century

Economic deficits may dominate our headlines, but ecological deficits will dominate our future.

—Lester Brown, *State of the World*, 1986

What is the status of the human at the close of the twentieth century? Although the Cold War has ended, military expenditures in many countries continue to match or exceed monies spent on education and health care. And although a commitment from over one hundred UN member nations to immunize 80% of the world's children by 1990 has now been achieved, children still continue to suffer unnecessarily from malnutrition, inadequate drinking water, and poor health care in many parts of the world. Structural poverty and gross inequalities of access to resources continue to prevent a majority of the world's population from enjoying amenities which are taken for granted by a privileged few. Wars between countries are on the decline, but civil and ethnic conflicts within states are increasing. Largely because of these conflicts, the refugee population throughout the world has reached its highest level since the end of World War II. These and other stark realities represent the context within which a majority of the world's population will likely greet the new millennium.

In sharp contrast to the above, a privileged minority of the world's population can look forward to a bright future—at least in the short term. The industrialized world seems to be on the verge of an information technology explosion that will see traditional conceptions of work, school, and leisure significantly transformed by what is being termed the information superhighway, a dizzying array of on-line computer services, multichannel TV universes, and shop-at-home networks. Furthermore, the trend toward lowered trade barriers between industrialized countries and the expansion of multinational companies into new international markets (often at the expense of poorer countries) could mean cheaper prices for consumer goods and services and the proliferation of new technologies and services in the marketplace.

Underlying the technological achievements of industrialized countries and the challenges faced by the developing world is a growing sense of urgency regarding the state of the global environment and the role of the human in contributing to disruptions in the ecological stability of the planet. Like many other publications that explore the ecological and cultural dimensions of the environmental crisis, the discussion that follows regards the current era to be a critical turning point in the relationship of the human to the natural world. It is argued that the decisions we make as a species and as members of a larger earth community in the next few decades will largely determine the long-term viability of our species and the planet as a whole.

There is a cautionary tale here, too, however. Steven Gelb (1991) points out that so-called apocalyptic prophecies and calls for cultural transformation arose not only in the present age, but also in ages past (perhaps especially at the dawn of a new century or millennium). For a myriad of reasons, but perhaps particularly because of scientific breakthroughs and political upheavals, many previous generations have also strongly (and sometimes mistakenly) believed that their respective eras would signal important turning points for human civilization. Gelb posits that "the egocentric belief that the present is unique and that the changes of our lifetime are precipitously new, different from anything that has occurred before" leads us to "inflate the importance of our ideas" (p. 40).

Although Gelb does not address the environmental crisis per se, such a perspective would seem to provide a different view of the critical importance of the present age, since the growing scarcity of resources, the degradation of land, water, and air, and global climatic changes we are witnessing at present *are* without precedence in human experience and largely reflect a biological/ecological view, rather than a cultural view of the world. The move from a cultural understanding of crisis (rooted in scientific breakthroughs and political upheavals, for example) to a biological/ecological view of crisis is significant because it grounds our understanding of crisis within the elementary powers of human perception, rather than complex interpretative accounts of the world. It means that while the cultural dimensions of the environmental impasse continue to be debated, there can be no denying the biological and ecological roots of our present predicament, as manifested in polluted lakes and rivers, depleted fish stocks, degraded croplands, and dying forest communities, among other examples. Only the precise magnitude and long-term ramifications of those practices which contribute to such devastation remain in dispute. To deny the environmental crisis in total, it is argued, would betray not only our better judgment, but also our basic powers of human perception.

With this in mind, the discussion below gives a brief overview of selected aspects of the biological and ecological crisis before moving on to explore specific interpretative accounts of the cultural dimensions of this crisis. An exploration of the multifaceted nature of the ecological challenge in terms of crises in economics and consciousness will help us in the next chapter to evaluate how the ideological aspects of contemporary calls for educational reform lead either to a "further intensification of" or "possible solutions to" the environmental impasse we currently face.

THE ENVIRONMENTAL IMPASSE AS A CRISIS OF ECOLOGY

It is the argument of this book that we have gradually eroded the life systems and ecological processes of the planet to such a degree that our present ways of living are no longer viable. Thomas Homer-Dixon and his associates (1993) describe the situation in these terms:

> Within the next 50 years, the human population is likely to exceed nine billion, and global economic output may quintuple. Largely as a result of these two trends, scarcities of renewable resources may increase sharply. The total area of highly productive agricultural land will drop, as will the extent of forests and the number of species they sustain. Future generations will also experience the ongoing depletion and degradation of aquifers, rivers and other bodies of water, the decline of fisheries, further stratospheric ozone loss and, perhaps, significant climate change. (p. 38)

From an ecological perspective, this situation has arisen because of disruptions in the ecological systems of biotic communities and the total global environment. Four key factors are highlighted in the passage above and briefly addressed below:

- exponential increases in the human population,
- the degradation of croplands, forest communities, aquifers, and other water bodies,
- ozone depletion and climatic change, and
- growing scarcities of resources and the extinction of species.

Overpopulation

The planet has reached the limit of its capacity to support human life, but the population of humans in many parts of the world continues to grow exponentially. Sharp increases in the rate of population growth are indicated by world trends over the last 400 years which show a population doubling time of 200 years in 1650, 80 years in 1850, 45 years in 1930, and just over 35 years at present (Ehrlich et al., 1973; Seager, 1995). While population growth rates are beginning to fall in some parts of the world, the overall global population nevertheless continues to increase. This is due in part to the sheer size of the global population at present. Other factors underlying this trend include increases in life expectancy and a sharp decline in incidence figures for many previously widespread diseases (e.g., smallpox and cholera). At present, a number of developing countries are expected to double in population in 25 years or less. However, these same countries will consume only a small fraction of the earth's resources, compared with industrialized nations which consume on a per capita basis as much as ten to fifteen times the resources as do developing countries. Other factors, as outlined below, also impact on the planet's inability to support steady increases in the human population. These include the degradation of croplands, shortages of clean water for drinking and agricultural use, and growing scarcities of resources.

The Degradation of Croplands, Forest Communities, and Water Bodies

We are witnessing at present the large-scale devastation of agricultural lands, forest communities, and water bodies throughout the world.

Croplands. Soil erosion and flooding due to vegetation loss is sharply reducing the per capita area of land available for sustained agricultural use. If present trends continue, it is estimated that by the year 2100, some 65% of the rain-fed croplands in the developing world will be lost due to soil erosion (UNICEF, 1989). Other factors such as deforestation, the overgrazing of livestock, and pollution due to air emissions and other waste products also impact the degradation of soil.

Forest Communities. At the current rate of deforestation, the world is at risk of losing virtually all its remaining tropical forests within the next forty years (Seager, 1995). Deforestation significantly reduces the complexity and biodiversity of forest communities essential for ensuring the long-term stability of ecosystems. The large-scale clear-cutting of forests can also lead to acute regional and global climatic change, imbalances in oxygen production, sharp decreases in precipitation, and increases in temperature on a global level. Monoculture agriculture in many of these cleared areas often involves the harvesting of only a few strains of productive crops, which further exasperates species loss. There are also human costs wrought by deforestation practices which threaten to dislocate Indigenous peoples from lands they have traditionally held for hundreds of years.

Water Bodies. Groundwater tables have steadily declined in many regions of the world, particularly in Africa, China, and India. At the other end of the spectrum, the erosion of soil causes runoff, which clogs rivers and lakes and increases the likelihood of flooding. Shortages of clean drinking water and water for irrigation purposes exist in many regions of the world and further threaten impoverished communities. The quality of existing water resources in industrialized countries is also threatened by industrial pollutants and other contaminants.

Ozone Depletion and Climatic Change

The layer of ozone in the earth's atmosphere prevents the most harmful forms of solar ultraviolet radiation from hitting the earth's surface. Although long-term trends for ozone depletion are not fully known, significant depletions in ozone levels, largely due to the release of CFCs (chlorofluorocarbons), have been recorded in recent years near both polar regions and densely populated regions of the world. Increases in the amount of ultraviolet radiation which pass through holes in the ozone layer can have a detrimental impact on the productivity of aquatic and terrestrial (land) ecosystems and lead to serious human health problems, including cancer, eye damage, and the suppression of immune systems. In addition to the above, an overdependence on fossil fuels, such as oil, natural gas, and especially coal, have created an imbalance in the release of carbon dioxide into the atmosphere. This has in turn contributed to a gradual warming of the earth's surface temperature (about .5°C) over the last 100 years (Ehrlich, 1991). Although speculative, the effects of this climate change could potentially cause severe alterations in rainfall patterns, sharp rises in sea level, more violent storms, and disruptions to coastal cities, vegetation, and wildlife habitat.

Resource Scarcity and Species Extinction

The major causes of animal extinction are overexploitation, loss of habitat (particularly through deforestation), hunting, and the luxury trade in animal skins and other organs. By the turn of the century, between 40,000 and 50,000 animal species a year could face extinction (Seager, 1995). Renewable and nonrenewable resources are also at risk of depletion. The sources of energy which have sustained industrial growth for over a century may also soon be totally exhausted (see Table 1.1). Other forms of resource scarcity extend from deforestation practices, strip-mining, and overfishing (e.g., the Canadian fisheries crisis in Newfoundland and British Columbia).

The points raised in the above discussion are indicative of only some of the factors that underlie the environmental impasse at present. A more

Table 1.1. Environmental and Inequitable Consequences of Current Economic Practices

The bracketed numbers in Figure 1.1 underscore four key areas where human economic practices further exasperate the environmental crisis and lead to gross inequalities of access to resources throughout the world:

1. *The depletion of natural resource stocks to unsustainable levels.* Presently, we are jeopardizing the resource base of the planet and new technological inventions are allowing us to extract resources at even greater rates. This applies to both renewable and nonrenewable resources. To take but one (albeit important) example: petroleum. Using data from the *International Energy Annual* (1988), Gregory A. Smith (1992) predicts future available oil supplies. Known oil reserves equal 990.6 billion barrels. World oil consumption in 1988 was 23.4 billion barrels. If expected increases in consumption rates and estimates on the discovery of new oil reserves are not taken into consideration the world has just 42 years of oil left; perhaps another 75 years or so if the latter estimates are factored in. Smith's conclusion is that "the long period of cheap and easily accessible energy that has sustained industrial development throughout the twentieth century is coming to an end" (p. 7).

2. *Over-consumption in the industrialized world.* The industrialized world comprises some 20% of the world's population, but consumes 80% of the earth's resources. Since World War II, there have been multifold increases in the consumption rates of resources and services in the world's richest countries, where a consumptive lifestyle is largely equated with human fulfillment. U.S. children on average hold more buying power than adults in the poorest countries (Durning, 1991).

3. *Gross disparities between peoples and between countries in the conditions of labor and distribution of goods and services.* In most countries, wealth continues to be concentrated in the hands of only a few. This is true for both developed and developing countries. In the United States, the richest 1% of the population controls 34.3% of the country's wealth. Throughout the world, the gap between rich and poor has widened from 3:1 in 1800 to 25:1 at present.

4. *Rising levels of pollution.* Despite new emission standards, increasing amounts of toxic pollutants continue to be released into the atmosphere in many countries. Yet the costs of pollution control measures for "heavily polluting industries"–large multinationals such as oil refineries, chemical companies, and auto manufacturers–are only between 1% and 2.5% of the total costs incurred by these industries (Cropper and Oates, 1992).

thorough review of these factors is given in the numerous UN and World-watch Institute reports that have been released over the past few years. The discussion below moves on from this biological/ecological focus to explore the cultural dimensions of the environmental crisis and begins by addressing how mainstream economic thought has typically misrepresented the resource scarcity question noted above.

THE ENVIRONMENTAL IMPASSE AS A CRISIS OF ECONOMICS

Traditional economic theory reduces control over natural resource scarcity to a single process—the price control mechanism. When a resource is plentiful, cheap prices reflect its abundance; when a resource becomes depleted, prices automatically increase to reflect its scarcity. In this way (so the thinking goes) a resource's abundance is always held in check and is never at risk of being totally eroded. There are variations on this thinking, however, which allow economists to discount the role of environmental scarcity in contributing to price control. Julien Simon (1981, p. 18), one of the most outspoken proponents of the price control mechanism, writes that "in general, then, if the scarcity of a raw material increases, its price will rise. But the converse need not be true; the price may rise even without a 'true' increase in scarcity." Here Simon's argument retains (for him) the best of both worlds. Falling prices indicate a plentiful resource. Rising prices do not necessarily imply a scarcity of resource. Hence allusions to environmental scarcities are not always made necessary by rising prices.

Although Simon's argument is written for the lay reader, it is founded on the same basic suppositions that have gained a general acceptance among a majority of economists. Most mainstream economists either ignore the environmental crisis altogether or, like Simon, place their *faith* in the infinite ability for human ingenuity, resourcefulness, and technological innovation to overcome all potential obstacles which might arise from dramatic environmental change. This optimism, while painting a rosy picture for the future, seems also to mask a deeper impatience with the environmental disruptions that have thrown traditional economic theory into disarray.

Figure 1.1 (adapted from Common, 1988) shows a typical flow diagram used by environmental economists to chart the passage of resources, goods and services, labor, and residuals (waste products) through the economy. On the left-hand side, the natural environment is both a source of inputs, or *natural resources*, to the production process and the ultimate dumping ground, or *depository*, for waste products. (*Amenities* refers to those aspects of the natural world which are consumed directly without going through the production process, such as living and recreational space

Figure 1.1. Environmental and Economic Flow Patterns (Adapted from Common, 1988, p. 13. Bracketed numbers refer to Table 1.1.)

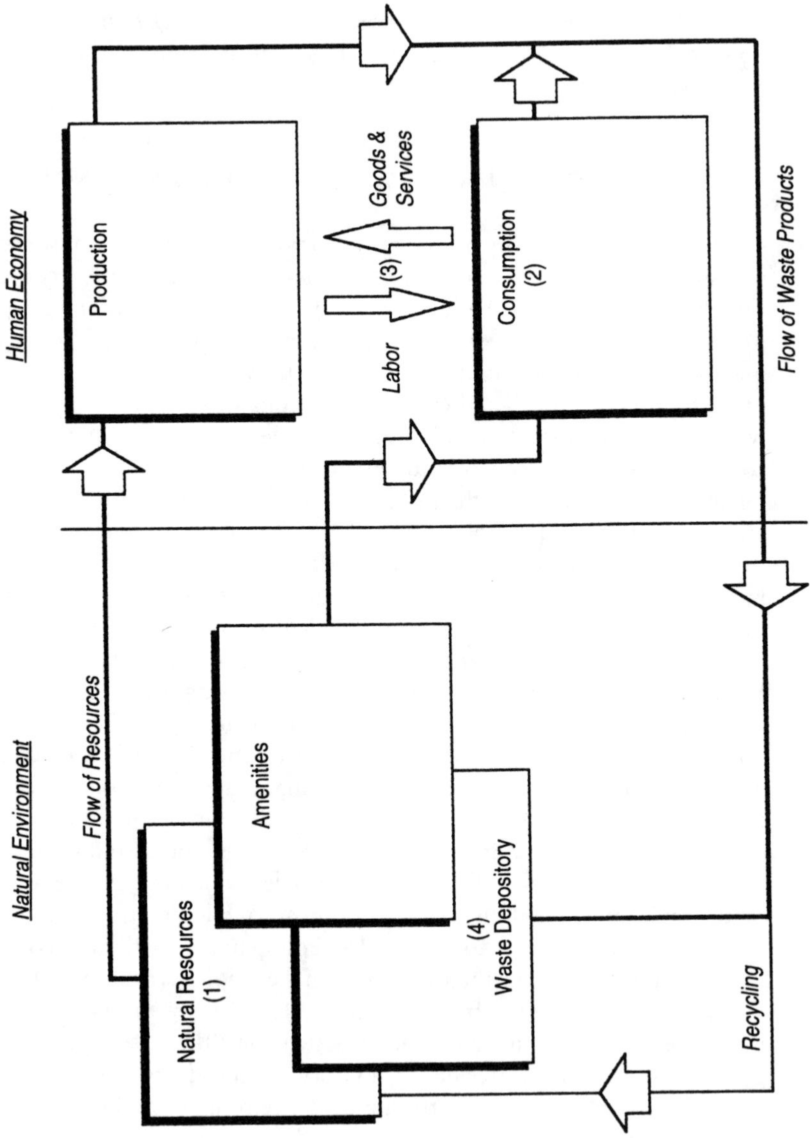

Human Economy

Production

Natural Environment

Flow of Resources

Goods &
Services

Labor

(3)

Consumption
(2)

Amenities

Natural Resources
(1)

(4)
Waste Depository

Recycling

Flow of Waste Products

and the beauty of the natural world itself.) On the right-hand side, the human economy comprises the two processes of production and consumption. *Production* refers to the manufacture of various products and commodities (both goods and services), which are then distributed for *consumption* (i.e., use) by consumers. Consumers also comprise the pool of labor supply (or *human capital*) for the production process itself. Hence the flow diagram shows a reciprocal relationship between the production and consumption processes to indicate the exchange of commodities and labor.

Most economists are concerned primarily with the human economy in general (the right side of the flow diagram) and the processes of production and consumption in particular. The input of resources from the natural world and output of waste products back into the natural world (the left side) are assumed and not given much thought beyond that. What is of concern are the conditions under which the greatest productivity (i.e., growth) of a human economy can occur as evident primarily through ever-increasing rates of consumption, an internationally competitive production process, and the development of new and more efficient technologies. The passages below give a clear sense of this passion for economic growth:

> [According] to most economists and politicians, unlimited expansion of the economy seems not only possible but desirable. Political leaders tout growth as the answer to unemployment, poverty, ailing industries, fiscal crises, and myriad other societal ills. To question the wisdom of growth seems almost blasphemous, so ingrained is it in popular thinking about how the world works. (Postel and Flavin, 1991, p. 186)

> Most governments, corporations, and voters assume that a healthy economy is one that uses increasing amounts of energy, materials, and resources to produce more goods, more jobs, and more income. This assumption dominates policies in energy, agriculture, and other resource sectors. It is a holdover from the mass economy of the industrial age, which was marked by a steady expansion in the production of energy, the depletion of resources, and the degradation of the environment. (MacNeill et al., 1991, p. 24)

> A nation living beyond its means faces precisely the same choice as a person living in the same manner; either it may grow poorer, or it may improve its means by becoming more productive. (Reich, 1990, p. 195)

The third quotation above is particularly revealing because in the first phrase, "a nation living beyond its means," the author seems to be indicating an awareness and concern for the unsustainability of traditional economic growth objectives; yet his final point on "increased productivity" betrays any such intent and necessarily implies a corresponding increase in resource exploitation and waste discharge as a way of increasing the flow of natural resources, commodities, and residuals through the economic system. Within such a context, the natural world is naively assumed to be somehow magically self-renewing in its ability to feed a competitive production machine and virtually limitless in its capacity to handle the waste products of an ever-expanding human economy. On a psychological level such naïveté is maintained in part by a disassociation or "splitting off" of a recognition of the inherent conditions of a finite natural world from the urgently perceived needs of a declining human economy.[1] Yet what Figure 1.1 shows us is that far from being distinct entities, the natural environment and human economy are intrinsically interrelated, particularly in terms of the "inputs to" and "outputs from" the production and consumption process. William Rees (1989) notes that

> industrial nations continue to act as if the economy operates in isolation from "the environment." The latter serves as an infinite storehouse of resources and sink for wastes, but is otherwise perceived as static, inert, and passive . . [but] the notion of environment as distinct entity is a sociocultural myth. Far from being separate, the environment and the economy have always been fully and inextricably integrated. The human economy is a wholly dependent sub-system of the ecosphere. (p. i)

It is significant that Rees sees the human economy as a subsystem of the natural world in contrast to both the vast majority of economists *and* Figure 1.1.[2] To take Rees's view implies the need for economic planning and policy-making to take their lead from a careful consideration of the needs of the wider earth community, rather than from a simple focus on human motives. The natural world establishes the context for the human economy; it establishes the basis upon which products and services are valued according to the degree that they enhance or degrade the biotic community as a whole. Within such a conception, economic planning and decision-making arise from a biocentric (rather than anthropocentric) view of the world, a shift in orientation which if heeded could begin to redress seriously these failings of traditional economic theory.

THE ENVIRONMENTAL IMPASSE AS A CRISIS OF CONSCIOUSNESS

Economic patterns of overconsumption and degradation of the environment have their roots in specific cultural assumptions which underlie our relations with the world. These assumptions serve as "cultural root metaphors" (Bowers, 1993), implicit belief structures which are *mythic* in origin, but aim to provide the human with a *functional* context for relating to the natural and physical worlds around us. Since the dawn of the modern age, these root metaphors have operated under the surface of consciousness in Western societies, often unacknowledged (and certainly unscrutinized) by most philosophers, scientists, and social commentators. At the root of these assumptions is a materialistic, rationalistic, and utilitarian view of nature which has in large part provided the conceptual validation for the human domination of the natural world throughout the modern age. Three specific assumptions and the impact of each on the cultural dimensions of the ecological crisis are next explored.

Notions of Time and Progress

The cultural construction of time emerges as one of the most powerful root metaphors of the modern industrial worldview. Within contemporary society, time is generally viewed as a linear process with a directionality that is forward moving, continuous, and progressive. Implicit to this idea of progressive change is the notion of a better, more advanced, and prosperous future life for later generations. Throughout modern history, this notion has found expression in a variety of ways: in the belief that science can eventually unlock all of nature's secrets (during the Enlightenment); in the notion of an ever-expanding human economy (in the Industrial Age); and in the contemporary belief that future technological innovations and human ingenuity will alone solve all human and environmental problems.

   Juxtaposed against this linear conception of time is the notion of cyclical time traditionally held by many Eastern and aboriginal cultures. Within these cultures "time" takes as its working metaphor not the idea of progress set forth above, but rather the cyclical quality of natural processes — seasonal transitions, the growth, decay, and rebirth of life, and the rhythm of the tides, among other examples. Within such a conception, the movement of time entails "a sequence of repeated acts of survival" (Berger, 1979, p. 203), the employment and reemployment of specific traditions and behaviors which have stood the test of time and are fundamentally "conserving" in their treatment of the natural world. Within such cultures, development entails the continual enhancement and differentiation of *existing* physical, symbolic, and cultural resources, rather than the stepped-up exploitation of untapped resources within the natural world.

Reductionism, Fragmentation, and Compartmentalization

The notion that the world can be best understood when it is broken down and dissected into its component parts extends from the seventeenth and eighteenth century scientific revolution in the West, of which the mechanistic worldviews advanced by Francis Bacon, Isaac Newton, René Descartes, and others are outgrowths. Implicit in this view is the notion of an atomistic world made up of discrete particles and the belief that all phenomena in nature can be best understood in isolation from each other. Although this line of thought finds expression within a variety of cultural contexts (including the arrangement of school curricula), its influence is most clearly evident within the traditions of "mechanistic science." Mechanistic science subscribes to the Newtonian–Cartesian conception which holds that the universe is composed of indestructible particles which are the fundamental building blocks of all matter. Atoms move in accordance with eternal and unalterable laws which, given enough time and investigation, can be fully explained using a mechanical model of the universe. Although the validity of the mechanistic worldview has long been rejected within the discipline of physics, it continues to exert a profound influence within the life sciences and the humanities.

Three essential characteristics of mechanistic science discredit it as the sole approach to the apprehension of knowledge. First, the reductionist tendencies of mechanistic science reveal its essential inadequacy as the basis for understanding the complexity of the world in which we live. The ultimate ambition of mechanistic science is to attribute all phenomena to as small a number of causes and constructs as possible. Hence much of what is not so easily explained by science risks being devalued, or worse yet, ignored altogether.

Second, the fragmentation of the world is invariably the price one pays when utilizing a scientific methodology, which out of necessity demands that interdependent phenomena be disconnected and isolated from each other in order to eliminate all confounding variables. Not only does this approach fail to take account of the essential relationships that exist between entities; it also violates the well-known axiom that the whole is far greater than the sum of its parts.

Finally, and closely related to the above, is the compartmentalization of what is perceived into separate and distinct categories, which invariably leads to the estrangement of the parts from the whole. As will be noted below, it is the separation of human from nature (or knower from known) which extends from this line of thought that contributes in large part to the conceptual validation of the subjugation of nature and the estrangement of the human from the natural world.

Such criticisms of mechanistic science are now gradually being countered by the more holistic approaches to scientific investigation adopted in recent years by a growing number of researchers working within the fields of ecology, biology, and quantum physics, among other disciplines. Within the holistic tradition there is a recognition that all phenomena exist interdependently with one other and cannot be fully understood except in relation to one another. (At a deeper level, some holistic theorists judge the mutual embeddedness and reciprocity of phenomena to be so complete that even the most inconspicuous of distinctions between phenomena is problematic.) Moreover, it is believed that consciousness may permeate matter in ways that were previously misunderstood or discounted. Working from such a perspective, many leading researchers within the holistic tradition (e.g., Bohm, 1983; Capra, 1975) have sought to break down the mind/matter dualism which has traditionally been at the root of scientific inquiry in the Western world.

Nature as Exploitable Resource

The notion that nature is an exploitable and expendable resource is so deeply ingrained in modern industrial culture that it is perhaps difficult to conceive of an alternative relationship between humans and the balance of the earth community. Florence Kluckhohn (1953) argues, however, that there are in fact three contrasting orientations which, throughout history, have variously underlain the relationship of the human to the natural world: the human as *subjugated to* nature; the human as *dominant over* nature; and the human as *an implicit part of* nature. In the first view, the natural world is judged to be all-powerful, unmanageable, and unpredictable and is often imbued with supernatural and demonic qualities. At the root of this orientation is the inability of the human to understand or regulate the natural world so that natural processes can be demystified and exploited for human purposes. Altman and Chemers (1980) argue that aspects of this orientation were evident in medieval societies, where the wilderness was judged to be foreboding and the personification of "evil."

The second orientation emerges in contrast and finds its origins in Western societies during the Scientific and Industrial revolutions some three centuries ago. Within this view, humans are judged superior to and masters over the natural world. Implicit in this orientation is the notion of the human as separate and removed from the natural world and not dependent on it for survival. Within such a design, nature is exploited for human benefit and has extrinsic value only in terms of its utility to the human. Current practices of deforestation and strip-mining can be traced to this view (as likely can the whole industrial enterprise itself). Scientific investigations play a special role within such an orientation and aim to "unlock nature's secrets" for the purpose of "harnessing nature" and "exploiting nature's untapped resources." This orientation presents a linear and progressive view of change in which social progress is equated largely with the further subjugation of the natural world and the development of newer and greater technological innovations based on this subjugation.

The third orientation is juxtaposed against the exploitation of the natural world. According to this orientation, people's lives—not only on a biological level, but also on a cultural and psychological level—are intertwined with the functioning of the natural world. From the perspective of this ecological view, "one cannot impose oneself on nature," write Altman and Chemers (1980, p. 21), "rather, one must flow with it, be part of it, understand its changing patterns . . . adapt to natural events . . . and work within its boundaries." Within this orientation the human is seen to be an implicit part of the natural world, inescapably connected with its workings, functioning, and ultimate destiny. Moreover, the human is judged to be only one of many species within the larger context of the earth community. It is a reciprocity between the human and the natural world, rather than human subservience to the natural world (or vice versa), which separates this perspective from the first and second orientations. Within this view, write Altman and Chemers, the natural world is

> [a] stable, orderly, and smoothly operating system. Events move in a systematic and cyclical fashion . . . seasons follow one another, natural events occur predictably, and people's lives flow in a clocklike and orderly way. Even life and death has a quality of harmony and cycling. (p. 21)

Although specific elements of each orientation find expression within the context of the environmental impasse, it seems clear that it is the second orientation—the human as dominant over nature—which is the most influential, since it not only establishes the context for the entire industrial enterprise of the present age, but also continues to strongly influence our notions of social progress.

TWO PATHS: TECHNOZOIC AND ECOZOIC

The above would seem to indicate that there *do exist* alternatives to present patterns of economic thought and exploitation of the natural world, but to move toward a more biocentric view of the natural world necessitates the need for:

1. economic planning and policy-making to take its lead from a careful consideration of the needs of the wider earth community, rather than a simple focus on human motives;

2. a new cyclical conception of time to take hold in which development entails the continual enhancement and differentiation of existing physical, symbolic, and cultural resources, rather than the stepped-up exploitation of untapped resources in the natural world;

3. a recognition of the interrelatedness of all phenomena in nature and the human impact on the natural world; and

4. a recognition that the human is an implicit part of the natural world, inescapably connected with its workings, functioning, and ultimate destiny.

These cultural reorientations (and most certainly others) would seem to be essential if the future viability of the earth community and the human species is to be assured.

That such a cultural reorientation will soon occur is not presently a foregone conclusion, however. As Brian Swimme and Thomas Berry (1992) argue, we are currently at a crossroads in our response to the ecological crisis. The choices we make as a species and as members of a larger earth community in the next few decades will largely determine whether we follow what they term a *Technozoic* path or an *Ecozoic* one:

> The future can be described in terms of the tension between the two forces [of the Technozoic and the Ecozoic]. If the dominant political–social issue of the twentieth century has been between the capitalist and the communist worlds, between democratic freedoms and socialist responsibility, the dominant issue of the immediate future will clearly be the tension between the Entrepreneur and the Ecologist, between those who would continue their plundering, and those who would truly preserve the natural world, between the mechanistic and the organic, between the world as a collection of objects and the world as a communion of subjects, between the anthropocentric and the biocentric norms of reality and value. (p. 250)

Implicit to the Technozoic path is a *faith* in the infinite ability for human ingenuity and technological innovation to solve all present and future human and environmental problems. This view forwards what James Robertson (1983) calls the "hyperexpansionist" option for the future, a belief that only a stepped-up expansion of the human economy and further exploitation of untapped resources can guarantee a viable future for post-industrial societies. As Robertson argues, exponents of this view hold that

> the human race, having expanded over every part of planet Earth since the 15th century, is now poised to colonize space; that scientific knowledge, having advanced ever more rapidly since the 16th and 17th centuries, is now about to capture the commanding heights of biology, psychology, communication and control; and that industrialism, having developed a dominating economic role since the 18th and 19th centuries, is now bringing super-industrial society to birth. A splendid future now beckons Western, scientific, industrial man if only he has the courage of his convictions. (p. 20)

The following statement by Bernard L. Cohen (1984) unabashedly reflects the technological optimism which is inherent to the Technozoic path outlined above, even despite the author's recognition of the environmental impasse:

> As a scientist I see no barriers to a bright future for America and for mankind. Irrespective of present trends, many minerals will eventually become more scarce and expensive, but we can develop substitutes for them. Food supply and environmental difficulties may well develop, but they can be solved. The only thing we need to handle these problems is an abundant and everlasting supply of cheap energy, and it is readily available in nuclear reactors, including the breeder. Given a rational and supportive public policy, science and technology can provide not only for the twenty-first century, but forever. (p. 556)

Within the Technozoic path, social progress is deemed to be synonymous with economic growth. By using science and technology more effectively, all current and future problems can be solved, if only we are determined and make effective use of the ultimate resource—the human mind. Implicit in this view is the gradual shift from a manufacturing and industrial–based economy to a high-technology and professional service–based economy. Although predictions for the future are inherently optimistic within the Technozoic path, they need to be accepted on the basis of faith, since the human ingenuity upon which this vision is founded does not yet exist. In other words, "it is not at all clear how the hyperexpansionist approach would break out of the [ecological] limits which . . . seem to be closing in on the developed economies of today" (Robertson, 1983, p. 22).

Juxtaposed against the Technozoic vision for the future is Swimme and Berry's (1992) notion of the Ecozoic age, an emerging era of human reengagement to the earth community and the most integral aspects of the natural world. Implicit in this path is a new valuation in the well-being of the entire biotic community, rather than an exclusive and myopic commitment to the well-being of the human. Most human institutions and cultural endeavors face cultural redefinitions, as we move from an anthropocentric view of the universe to a more ecological and biocentric conception which recognizes the dependency (and interdependency) of the human on the healthy functioning of the natural world.

A deep awareness of the sacred, founded on the notion of the earth and universe as a onetime endowment—a chance coming together of disparate forces—emerges as a primary celebratory experience for the human within the Ecozoic age. Similarly, it is a *reciprocity* within and between the natural and cultural worlds of the human and the balance of the earth community which establishes the context for all forms of human achievement and cultural expression. Living supportively with one another and with the balance of the earth community emerges as a major goal during this period of human reconciliation with the natural world.

Swimme and Berry argue that the early stages of the transition to an Ecozoic age are evident at present in the basic strivings of the environmental, peace, and other contemporary social movements. The task at present is to relate the ecological wisdom of these movements to all areas of cultural and institutional life. There needs to be a new recognition within the medical profession, for example, that the well-being of the human is intricately related to and dependent on the health of the planet. Similarly, our religious traditions need to foster a new "subjective communion" with the various elements of the biotic community, and notions of justice within the legal profession need to begin to address the protective needs of the wider earth community.

As will be suggested in the next chapter, this reformulation also extends to the educational domain, especially in terms of the types of knowledge, attitudes, and values that are explicitly and implicitly reinforced within schools. Chapter 2 considers some of the environmentally "sensitive" versus "problematic" elements of three contemporary philosophies of education, two of which currently inform much of the public debate on matters relating to schooling. A key question is posed: *How do the ideological aspects of contemporary calls for educational reform lead either to a "further intensification of" or "possible solutions to" the environmental impasse which we currently face?*

CHAPTER 2

Toward a Twenty-First Century Pedagogy of Possibility

Education [is] the battleground upon which the most significant social conflict [has taken] place in the twentieth century.
— Clarence J. Karier, *The Individual, Society, and Education: A History of American Educational Ideas* (1986)

Environmental education curricula and outdoor experiential programs constitute the largest proportion of attempts by educators to address the environmental crisis and explore human/earth relations with students. In addition to the traditional nature study program comprising the requisite pond study and Ph test, it is possible to distinguish among at least three other popular approaches to environmental education. The *supplemental* approach comprises discrete learning activities which are typically designed for use by classroom teachers who have little or no background experience in environmental education, but who may be interested in conducting an occasional experiential or outdoor activity with their students. Supplemental approaches, such as the popular *Project Learning Tree* program in the United States and *Project Wild* in Canada, demand little in the way of lesson preparation or financial/curricular resources and are relatively nonobtrusive as regards the normal agenda of schools.

The supplemental approach can be contrasted with the *infusionist* approach, in which environmental themes and subject matter are integrated into existing traditional subjects such as mathematics, geography, and science. Such an approach gives prominence to environmental issues and aims to help students gain a wider understanding of these issues and their relationship to traditional subject areas. Two outcomes of this approach have been a proliferation of curricula on environmental issues and the founding of a small number of environmentally focused public schools throughout North America.

The success of the supplemental approach in designing curricula for

24

teachers with little experience in environmental education and the infusionist approach in bringing environmental issues to the fore in traditional school subjects has not left either approach without its critics. For example, Steve Van Matre (1990) has launched a virulent attack on both models of environmental education, focusing particularly on their failure to develop "focused, sequential instructional programs" (p. 4). He advocates what might be described as an *intensive experience* approach to environmental education in which students participate in a carefully crafted two- or three-day residential environmental education program away from their regular studies. He argues that even a short intensive experience program, when effectively designed and followed up, can have a greater impact on students than a longer series of disconnected environmental activities (his caricature of the supplemental approach) or a fragmented curriculum sprinkled with environmental themes and messages (his caricature of the infusionist approach).

Despite Van Matre's enthusiasm for the intensive experience approach, an important question remains as to whether any of these three approaches can actually leave a lasting impression on students. A definitive answer is not yet possible, since few studies have been conducted to determine the long-term effects of environmental education programs on the knowledge retention or the values/attitudinal/lifestyle changes evoked in students. From a less than optimistic viewpoint, gains made by any of these approaches are likely to be undercut by the dominant industrial ethos of schools in which environmental education plays but a minimal role. Hence the compartmentalized nature of the curriculum of most schools overshadows the need to nurture an ecological view of the world. Similarly, the need to nurture an ethic of ecological sensitivity is obscured in many if not most courses by the notion of nature as exploitable resource. As Stevenson (1987, p. 74) argues, the transformative goals of environmental education largely work against "the traditional purpose of schools . . . of conserving the existing social order by reproducing the norms and values that currently dominate environmental decision-making. Therein lies the first major contradiction between environmental education and schooling."

Even seemingly well-intentioned efforts to nurture an environmental awareness in schools can fall victim to habitual ways of thinking. The following activity is taken from a grade five environmental curriculum guide. It begins as a well-meaning exercise in taxonomy, but ends up not-so-subtly reinforcing ecologically questionable values related to property and ownership:

> *Staking a Claim*: Divide the group into teams of 4 or 5 each . . . Each team stakes out a claim [of a natural space] using a piece of string about 6 yards long and with both ends joined . . . The object is to see how many different things

students can find in the claim. Members of the team report each find to [an appointed] secretary who writes it down . . . Each team "owns" everything over its claim, the branch of a tree, [the] blue sky. If a cloud passes over the claim it may be counted. If a fly goes over it, a bird, or, if a beetle walks in . . . these may be written down. The team also "owns" the ground under the claim and may dig in it with their hands or a stick if they like . . . After time is called the teams visit each other's claims and hear the secretary's report. (Scarborough Board of Education, 1988, p. 79)

If we are to effectively counter the ecologically problematic aspects of curriculum and schooling, what seems most important is an assessment of the underlying ideological assumptions which inform educational practice and surreptitiously influence the lives of students and educators on a daily basis. When made overt, these assumptions form what might be described as an *educational philosophy*, a set of explicit beliefs about the nature of the educative process itself. In a general sense, an educational philosophy provides answers to questions relating to the purpose of education, the role of the school in society, and our obligations to future generations. It further makes clear the roles to be fulfilled by teacher and student, indicates what aspects of a student's life are within the mandate of the school or learning situation, and (often subtly) dictates whose values will dominate the educational process itself.

THREE PHILOSOPHIES APPLIED TO EDUCATION: TECHNOCRATIC, PROGRESSIVE, AND HOLISTIC

This chapter reviews and critiques three contemporary philosophies of education (see Table 2.1). Proponents of the *technocratic* philosophy argue that the declining health of the American, Canadian, and other industrialized economies necessitates a return to a basic program of instruction and a renewed commitment to higher standards of educational attainment. Supporters of *progressive* education argue for an inquiry-based approach to learning which fosters an experimental temperament in students. Proponents of the *holistic* philosophy stress the child's search for meaningfulness and purpose in the physical and cultural worlds which surround the child.

Special attention is paid to the ideological roots of each of the three philosophies which lead either to a further intensification of or possible solutions to the environmental impasse we currently face. Although it is a primary aim of this book to outline an ecologically sensitive approach to education, none of the three philosophies is critiqued solely from an environmental perspective. Rather, the focus is on those objections which can be raised against each of the three positions from a variety of contexts.

It is important to note that the philosophies reviewed below represent only a small minority of the numerous perspectives competing for attention in the debate over educational reform. Other contrasting positions are forwarded by the emancipatory and critical education movement, behaviorism, various Eastern philosophies, and the liberationist movement, among others. Although these philosophies do not figure prominently in what follows, specific elements of each do make their way into the discussion of this and later chapters. Of particular significance is Howard Gardner's argument (1991) that the primary purpose of education should be for disciplinary initiation. Also significant are the efforts of some neoconservative writers, such as Neil Postman (1984), who seek to remedy their particular assessment of our "cultural crisis" through a reactionary program of educational reform. Although Postman's more recent proposals for education (1995) actively embrace an environmental ethic, his early views on education remain no less important for consideration:

> I am proposing a curriculum in which all subjects are presented as a stage in humanity's historical development, in which the philosophy of science, of history, of language, and of religion are taught, and in which there is strong emphasis on classical forms of artistic expression. Such an education might be considered conservative. But I believe it is justified by the fact that we are surrounded by a culture that is volatile, experimental, and very nearly monolithic in its technological biases. Without the schools to teach the values and intellectual predispositions that out media ignore, and even despise, our students will be disarmed and their future exceedingly bleak. (1984, p. 223)

Despite a wide range of competing perspectives in education, it is clearly the technocratic and progressive philosophies which have dominated the public discourse on educational reform in recent years and throughout most of the twentieth century. Indeed, on a rudimentary level, it may in fact be possible to chart the history of educational reform as a series of skirmishes between the technocratic and progressive camps. We often speak of the "swinging of the pendulum" to describe the process by which these two competing ideologies contest gains made by the other and attempt to influence public opinion. In both the United States and Canada the popular media have tended to dichotomize the debate over the fundamental aims of schooling, pitting the merits of the technocratic call for a renewed focus on basic skills against the progressive philosophy's attention to the needs of the individual child.

Significantly, it is the technocratic philosophy itself which establishes the context not only for much of the recent public discourse on educational reform, but also the historical legacy of schools themselves. Many of the current proposals for reform (from the self-proclaimed "education for excel-

Table 2.1. Three Philosophies Applied to Education
(Compiled with reference to John P. Miller and Wayne Seller, 1985; John P. Miller, 1988; and Sue Greig et al., 1989.)

Selected Aspects	Technocratic "Back to Basics" Education	Progressive "Child-centered" Education	Holistic Education
1. Foremost aim	To help students develop the knowledge, skills, and values they will need in order to secure productive jobs and participate in a competitive marketplace.	To help students develop the knowledge, skills, and values they will need in order to participate effectively as citizens within a democratic society.	To help students develop the knowledge, skills, and values they will need in order to further their personal growth beyond formal schooling and respond effectively to dramatic global change.
2. Years of influence	The dominant philosophy of institutionalized mass schooling in North America from its original inception in the mid-18th century until the present moment. In recent years, the consistently poor performance of North American students on standardized international tests has provoked a renewed call for improvements in the teaching of basic literacy and numeracy skills, particularly from parents, universities, and the business community. This has in turn prompted the greater involvement of the business community itself in matters relating to education.[2]	Reaction to the anti-democratic nature of schooling in the early twentieth century and the rise of John Dewey's pragmatic philosophy of education marked its first wave of influence.[6] A second wave occurred alongside the rise of humanistic psychology in the early 1970s, through a (somewhat dubious[7]) association with the free-school movement (e.g. Summerhill), and in response to a proliferation of scathing critiques of technocratic education (e.g. by John Holt).	Although in many ways a recent phenomenon, holistic education can trace its historical roots back to the nineteenth century educational endeavours of Friedrich Froebel (founder of the kindergarten) and the twentieth century educational movements pioneered by Maria Montessori and Rudolf Steiner. In recent years, holistic education has forged ties with the peace and environmental movements and turned to the findings of quantum physics and ecology to corroborate its approach to education.

3. Spheres of influence	Pervades the entire curriculum, particularly at the secondary level. Proponents argue that it is especially conducive to the effective teaching of reading, writing, and math. Proposes the phonics approach to the teaching of literacy in elementary school.	The dominant philosophy for the earliest years of schooling (kindergarten through grades 2 or 3). Proposes the whole-language approach to the teaching of literacy in elementary school. (This can also be viewed as a holistic education proposal.)	Being a recent phenomenon, its influence so far has been primarily limited to various independent and public alternative schools, gifted classes, secondary school courses, and global education curricula.
4. Basic worldview	*Atomistic:* The universe is made up of discrete particles. All phenomena can be understood in isolation from each other. Reductionistic and mechanistic science can best explain the world.	*Pragmatic:* The universe is in a continuous state of process and flux. All phenomena can be understood by applying the scientific method. Through reflective experience we can explain the world.	*Organic:* The universe is made up of interconnected parts and systems. All phenomena can only be fully understood in relation to each other and in relation to the larger system or whole of which it is apart. A focus on whole systems can best explain the world.
5. View of the natural world	*Exploitive:* The human is divorced from the natural world and is not dependent on it for survival. Nature has extrinsic value only in terms of its utility to the human. Technology and human ingenuity alone can solve our "greatly exaggerated" environmental crisis.[3]	*Benevolent:* The human is the caretaker of the natural world. Legislation, combined with the rational use of natural resources and science and technology, can solve our environmental problems. Stewardship is stressed as an environmental ethic.	*Participatory:* The human is an implicit part of the natural world, inescapably connected with its workings, functioning, and ultimate destiny. On both an individual and species level, there is a desperate need for us to curb our destructive impact on the planet.

Table 2.1. Three Philosophies Applied to Education
(Compiled with reference to John P. Miller and Wayne Seller, 1985; John P. Miller, 1988; and Sue Greig et al., 1989.)

Selected Aspects	Technocratic "Back to Basics" Education	Progressive "Child-centered" Education	Holistic Education
6. View of social change	Social change occurs through the efforts of successful individuals who hold power and prestige. Effective change increases human amenities, aims for greater organizational efficiency, and spurs on technological development.	Social change is managed in a rational and scientific manner through participatory processes of community decision-making. Effective change can only succeed within the context of a democratic society.	Social change aims to improve the functioning of the whole system and not only individual components thereof. Only by squarely facing ingrained cultural and institutional practices can effective change occur.
7. Dimensions of consciousness emphasized	An almost exclusive focus on the cognitive dimension	Balances the cognitive and affective dimensions.[8]	Balances the cognitive, affective, and spiritual dimensions and seeks to build connections between them.
8. Notions of development in childhood	Differences between adults and children (in terms of cognitive functioning, learning processes, and ways of seeing the world) are judged to be minimal. This translates into few differences in instructional methodology between the elementary and secondary levels, save for the earliest years of schooling.	A strong emphasis on the social and intellectual development of the child. A concern for the social adjustment of the child to school community and peer group and an allegiance to Piagetian-inspired notions of cognitive development.	A strong emphasis on the social, intellectual, and spiritual development of the child. A focus on the child's developing relationship to the world, especially the natural world. A concern for the "whole child," including the developmental role played by various physiological systems other than the brain and nervous system (e.g., the limb and respiratory systems).

	Transmission	Transaction	Transformation
9. Curriculum orientation[1] and instructional design	*Transmission:* Learning mainly occurs through a one-way dissemination of knowledge from teacher to student. A focus on rote memorization, mastery learning, and critical thinking skills.[4]	*Transaction:* Learning occurs through a two-way interaction between the student and the curriculum, teacher, and peer group. A focus on problem-solving skills, learning strategies, cooperative learning and social skills/self-esteem building.	*Transformation:* Learning occurs through a process of personal and social development. A focus on personal growth, learning styles, and critical thinking skills leading to social and attitudinal change.
10. Subject integration	The curriculum is subject based and allows for little or no subject integration or cross-disciplinary learning. The sovereignty of segregated disciplines is paramount.	The curriculum is subject based, but allows for some interdisciplinary and theme-based subject integration, especially at the elementary level	The curriculum is theme-based and transdisciplinary. Traditional subject boundaries are judged as arbitrary and seen to promote a fragmented instructional program.
11. Values education	Little or no explicit programming of values education. Judges schools to be value-free and nonpartisan and stridently strives to protect this status. (Implicitly, the curriculum aims to preserve the status quo and is generally saturated with a strong business ethic.[5]	Emphasizes a values clarification approach and stresses strategies for cooperative (group) learning. Focuses on those social amenities that sustain a democratic society such as sharing and respect for individual differences.	Nurtures an ethic of caring which extends beyond the student's immediate environments to also embrace other peoples and cultures, and beyond the human world to also embrace the natural world.
12. Primary methods of evaluation	Standardized quantitative assessment (i.e. tests). Focus on product (outcomes). Supports comparative testing between schools and between countries.	Anecdotal qualitative observations of the student, especially in early elementary school. Focus on process (learning strategies). Also some self and group evaluation.	As with progressive education, but a somewhat greater emphasis on non-formal forms of self and group evaluation.

Table 2.1. Three Philosophies Applied to Education

(Compiled with reference to John P. Miller and Wayne Seller, 1985; John P. Miller, 1988; and Sue Greig et al., 1989.)

Notes

[1] Differences in curriculum orientation are discussed in detail in Miller and Seller (1985).

[2] For a general critique of this involvement see McMurtry (1989). Strong objections have also been raised against industry-produced "newscasts" for students (e.g. Suzuki, 1992) and the proliferation of industry-produced curricula and other materials into the schools (e.g. Link-Brenkman, 1983).

[3] For the argument behind this view see Simon (1981) and my discussion of the Technozoic vision in Chapter 1.

[4] This last focus is a relatively recent phenomenon, set in motion in response to new instructional directives from the business community. Critical thinking from this perspective should not be confused with critical thinking leading to social change. Within technocratic education, the "boundaries" for critical thinking are clear to all, and any transgression of these boundaries is sharply censured, so as not to challenge the "dominant values" of society (e.g. that strong business ethic referred to above).

[5] Some technocratic educators make this ethic explicit. They argue that schools should stress values such as social conformity, (noncritical) obedience to authority, and self-reliance and nurture a competitive spirit between students to inculcate these values.

[6] For a historical overview of the early years of the progressive school movement see Cremin (1982). As I note in Chapter 2, the progressive education movement successfully appropriated certain facets of Dewey's thought, but misrepresented other aspects.

[7] Generally speaking, the free-school movement embraced an anti-intellectual stance which, in the view of Aronowitz and Giroux (1993), helped propel the rise of the technocratic call for reform.

[8] Some critics describe the progressive (and holistic) philosophies as "feel good education" and claim they overemphasize the affective dimension. For example, see Krauthammer (1990).

lence" movement, for example) are founded on the same basic principles of social cohesion and standardization of curriculum that first characterized the development of schools in the mid-nineteenth century. As Pulliam (1987) notes:

> [The] school system was designed in the early national period under the leadership of school reformers like Horace Mann [and Eggerton Ryerson in Canada] . . . The nation then was dominated by agriculture, making a common school with summer vacations and local control quite acceptable. With the rise of industry, standardization of the curriculum and a delivery system based on a Newtonian mechanistic model was adopted. The school system became a closed machine with top-down administration, predetermined standards, lockstep definitions of content by grade, and fixed rules of behavior. Obviously the system worked well to prepare students for the factory or the office. With its emphasis on assimilation, conformity, and traditional values, it was able to handle the masses of European immigrants and the growing [North] American population. Mass production philosophy and assembly line concepts lent themselves to efficiency in the production of trained workers at low cost. (p. 241)

Both the progressive and holistic calls for educational reform find their roots within an adverse reaction to the historical precedents first established by technocratic proponents in the mid-nineteenth century. The basis for each of these two philosophies arises from a consideration of the perceived failings of technocratic education. In this sense, the progressive and holistic reform movements have relied as much on the effectiveness of their critique of technocratic education as on the constructivist elements of their respective philosophies.

ECONOMICS AND EDUCATION: THE TECHNOCRATIC PHILOSOPHY

The educational movement calling for technocratic reform in schools can trace its historical roots back to nineteenth and early-twentieth century attempts to streamline curriculum, bring schools in line with the changing needs of business and industry, and ensure efficiency of operation. In recent decades this movement has been provoked not by a single incident (such as the 1957 Soviet launching of Sputnik caused), but by a series of perceived social and economic crises affecting the industrialized world as a whole, and North America in particular. These include our transition to a postindustrial society, an increase in international economic competition, and the decline in the educational standards of schools and the basic literacy, numeracy, and thinking skills of children and adults. Each of these phenomena are briefly considered in turn.

Proponents of the technocratic philosophy argue that we are currently "in the midst of a cultural and economic revolution that parallels that of the Industrial revolution of the past century" (DeYoung, 1989, p. 99). The social and economic upheaval that we are presently experiencing is (at least in part) symptomatic of this revolution. Such a shift is marked by our transition from a labor-intensive and industrial-based economy to a technology-intensive and information-based economy. More specifically, the technologization and automation of the workplace and replacement of low-skill jobs in factories and other sectors with computers and robots has severely curtailed the demand for low-skilled laborers in recent years. Yet this trend has been offset by significant increases in the number of high-skill and maintenance jobs currently being created to service and maintain this technology and research and develop new technologies.

Since, from the technocratic perspective, schools should play an important role in the development of occupational skills, it stands to reason that the primary efforts of our educational system should be aimed at following the path laid out by shifts in demographic and employment trend indicators associated with our transition to a postindustrial society. Hence the first obligation of schools is to ensure the future employability of all students by graduating highly skilled business people, scientists, technicians, and other workers. Within such occupations, flexibility in skill will be an important criterion of career success, since most workers will be required to change occupations several times during their lives as old technologies quickly become obsolete and are replaced by newer technological innovations in a rapidly modernizing postindustrial society.

Closely allied with our transition to a postindustrial society is the globalization of the world's economies and the growing complexity of international trade relations between nations. A primary concern of technocratic proponents is the role that increased international competitiveness (particularly from Japan and Germany) is playing in slowing down the economic growth and productivity of the American and Canadian economies. By focusing on economic trend data detailing trade deficits and declining rather than growing productivity levels, technocratic proponents argue that we are currently being outperformed by our international competitors. Since schools are a primary agent for the development of occupational skills, we can turn to public education to find the roots of this crisis. By closely attending to what other countries are doing "right" with their schools, we can adapt our educational system to better reflect the needs of our economic system and gradually turn trade deficit/surplus and productivity levels to our advantage.

Technocratic proponents argue that the fight for a competitive edge internationally should begin at school and set the agenda for public education. Hence, in the name of efficiency and excellence, many of their reform proposals involve changing schools to better reflect the organizational climate of industry and business. As Kearns and Doyle (1988) readily agree, "the new agenda for school reform will be driven by competition and market discipline, unfamiliar ground for educators" (p. 140).

International comparisons between schools are taken one step further as technocratic proponents link their calls for reform to the often disappointing results of international achievement tests assessing the basic knowledge of students in a variety of subject areas (especially the maths and sciences). Compared to our international competitors, North American students consistently perform below average on these tests, and such poor results are interpreted by technocratic proponents to be an indication of the failure of public education to successfully teach basic literacy, numeracy, and problem-solving skills. Such conclusions are reinforced by calls for reform from employers and representatives of postsecondary institutions who argue that the public schools are sending them increasing numbers of illiterate students.

This indictment of our public schools has given rise to a variety of scathing critiques of North American education in recent years. Since 1983, numerous government and business reports have called for a "total overhaul" and "massive restructuring" of the schooling process in both the United States and Canada based on the charge that schools are failing to adequately prepare young people for the challenges of a competitive global marketplace. Typically subsumed within a discourse of crisis, these reports have argued that only a drastic shift in the educational priorities of our public schools from concerns over educational *equality* to concerns over educational *quality* (see Aronowitz and Giroux, 1993, p. 16) will be able to secure the economic future of North America and ensure the future employability of its students. An excerpt of the recommendations for one such U.S. report reads as follows:

> [We call for] the reassessment and realignment of school curricula, imposing higher expectations and more rigorous standards for student behavior and accomplishment, developing appropriate and accurate performance measures, and providing insights from business management that can assist schools in developing an organizational climate that supports improvement. (Committee for Economic Development, 1985, p. 6)

While the conclusions reached by this and other publications vary from report to report, almost all are united in several key recommendations. These include the call for a curriculum of core subjects which stress academic over "nonacademic" content (e.g., the sciences over the arts); higher academic standards in all subject areas; standardized testing at regular intervals, beginning early in elementary school; a forging of links between schools and business; and a higher quality of teacher education with more training hours devoted to subject content rather than teaching methodology.

Criticisms of the Technocratic Perspective

Proponents of the technocratic perspective have been largely successful in mobilizing public discontent against the schools. At first glance, this philosophy seems to address the fears and concerns of many people whose livelihoods and futures are presently being jeopardized by economic uncertainty, but the focus seems to be less on the equitable distribution of national wealth in the United States and Canada and more on strategies for rebuilding the threatened infrastructure of big business and industry. Referring to this technocratic mindset, Herman Daly (1989, p. 74) writes that "the growth ideology is extremely attractive politically because it offers a solution to poverty without requiring the moral discipline of sharing." Similarly, Alexander Lockhart (1977, p. 79) notes that the technocratic position promises "not only high levels of national economic success . . . but also high levels of individual social mobility in the up direction *without* implying any threat of downward mobility for the already privileged." Yet despite its surface attractiveness, a number of serious objections can be raised against the technocratic argument for educational reform.

First, it is not clear that the years ahead will see a dramatic increase in the number of high-skill jobs as technocratic proponents predict—certainly not enough to offset the large number of low-skill job positions which are vacated. Technocratic proponents use occupational data to support their argument, but as Bailey (1991) points out, occupational data has been used to make a case both for and against the upgrading of skill requirements of jobs. Hadlock, Hecker, and Gannon (1991), for example, use U.S. Bureau of Labor Statistics to contradict the technocratic position and predict slower than average growth projections for high-skill jobs through to the year 2000. Further to this, Carnoy (1987) argues that the net effect of the technologization of the workplace is to reduce, not increase the skill and knowledge requirements of most jobs. And more recently, Jeremy Rifkin (1995) has called into serious question the ability of the dawning postindustrial age to provide high-skilled job opportunities for more than a small fraction of the work force. Although employment projections are not always accurate (Bailey, 1991) and forecasts of slow high-skill job growth have been disputed (e.g., by Bishop and Carter, 1991), it is questionable whether projections of any sort should be the determining factor in setting the agenda for public education. And beyond all the figures is the (often overlooked) reality that a declining resource base associated with environmental degradation may soon make long-term projections of any sort unreliable.

In addition to these statistical criticisms, the technocratic philosophy can also be called into question on the basis of specific ideological weaknesses. Similar to the Technozoic vision outlined in Chapter 1, technocratic proponents base their argument on antiquated nineteenth and early twentieth century notions of social progress which are no longer viable, given the global realities of the present age. Within the technocratic philosophy, "social progress" is deemed to be synonymous with "economic growth," and "the only limit to growth is believed to be a chronic shortage of highly and specifically educated manpower" (Lockhart, 1977, p. 78). Yet at the same time that these arguments are being forwarded, we are faced with a global environmental crisis that threatens traditional notions of progress that are equated with an ever-expanding human economy. Environmental economists such as Herman Daly (1989) are fervently arguing that we need to work toward a new definition of economic development, one in which the *quality* of economic production is valued over *quantity* of economic activity.[1] In sharp contrast, the technocratic philosophy posits unchecked economic growth as the *only* way to a brighter future for the United States and Canada.

The technocratic philosophy does not simply miss the mark on matters relating to the declining health of the planet; it fosters the very mystique that has led to this impasse in the first place. Technocratic proponents clearly identify specific challenges facing industrialized communities at present, but the wider cultural (and ecological) dimensions of these challenges are virtually ignored. In general, then, technocratic proponents agree with environmentalists that we are presently in the midst of a cultural crisis, but they take a peculiarly limited view of what that crisis might entail.

One further way of framing the ideological limitations of the technocratic position is to recognize that its reform proposals are fuelled almost wholly by the motives of industry and business, and that these motives do not adequately reflect (indeed, they often run contrary to) many of the traditional commitments and obligations of public schools. Education provides basic socialization related to community living and participation in a democratic society, while the basic impulse of business and industry is to maximize profits while minimizing contributions to the public good. This is particularly true of large-scale multinational corporations (representatives of which are strong proponents of technocratic education) which develop few allegiances or commitments to the well-being of communities and individuals outside of the profit motives of the company.[2] Hunt (1988) characterizes the situation in this way:

[A] substantial anomaly exists in the relationships between societies and the major producers of goods and services . . . it usually turns out that the productive system of a society is composed substantially of larger corporations that are multinational in character and foreign-based . . . their presence is only incidentally to contribute to the well-being of the host society, rather, their primacy of concern with growth and profits, and lack of commitment to any particular society, gives rise to a search for cheaper materials, lower wages, taxes and other charges, minimal constraints on their operations, and better markets . . . it is they, too, which employ the more predatory and other anti-social strategies, particularly when under challenge for market position, profits, or other objectives . . . as a basic group into which people are born and socialized, societies provide health, education, social, and other services for their development and well-being. In contrast, corporations have taken over the profit-making, productive process, and sought to dissociate themselves from societies, even to minimize their contributions to public resources . . . so, on the one hand, there is the politically and socially grouped citizenry constituting communities and societies, and on the other, corporations pursuing growth and profits across societies. (pp. 138, 140)

It follows from these criticisms that the technocratic philosophy seriously limits the potential role that public education can play in further strengthening democratic and community life in American and Canadian societies. (Indeed, the very concept of community is irritably altered within the context of the technocratic philosophy as networks of individuals linked by global telecommunications replace face-to-face interactions between people within local communities.) By promoting the interests of business and private enterprise over other, more community-oriented concerns, such as citizenship education and local community-based decision-making, technocratic proposals severely curtail the role that schools can play as critical spheres of public discourse. While technocratic proponents may pay lip service to the educational goals of instilling democratic and community values in students, their efforts actually appear to be aimed at streamlining curriculum and injecting market discipline into schools, reforms that arguably work against the educational requirements of a democratic society.

This last point can be seen clearly in many of the business and government educational reports calling for technocratic reform in schools. Typically, such reports begin with a laudable statement emphasizing the contributions of schools to cultural and democratic ideals, but the discussion soon shifts to a restricted focus on the "economics of education" literature and obligations of schools to the North American industrial order. A 1992 report from *The Economic Council of Canada* opens with this statement, for example:

> Education is the very lifeblood of society, sustaining our endeavors and shaping our prospects. Not only do good citizenship and the democratic ideal depend on a well-informed and well-educated citizenry, but the learning process also makes a critical contribution to creativity and intellectual curiosity. (p. 1)

It seems unlikely that "creativity" and "intellectual curiosity" can be effectively nurtured through an exclusive focus on basic and technical skills, yet this is precisely what the balance of the report advocates. Although the same publication recognizes "that our focus is primarily economic [and] that the formal education system, in particular, has a range of valuable objectives that are just as important—some might argue, more important" (p. 3), it goes on to suggest that among other reforms, schools should offer "a limited number of key subjects, with very few electives" (p. 16) and that a primary commitment of teachers should be to "respond to employers' needs" (p. 48).

By streamlining curricula for the sole purpose of fulfilling labor market imperatives, technocratic reform proposals aim to severely curtail the mandate of schools within a democratic society. In defiance of the more traditional concerns of schools for instilling "moral and character development" and ensuring "equality of opportunity," the technocratic philosophy argues that responding to the needs of employers should be the primary *or even sole* responsibility of public education. Writing in the foreword to David Purpel's book *The Moral and Spiritual Crisis in Education* (1989), Henry Giroux and Paulo Freire underscore this assessment:

> Under the guise of attempting to revitalize the language of morality, right-wing educators and politicians have, in reality, launched a dangerous attack on some of the most fundamental aspects of democratic public life and the obligations of socially responsible critical citizenship. What has been valorized in this ideological discourse is not the issue of reclaiming public schools as agencies of social justice and critical democracy, but an elitist view of schooling based on a celebration of cultural uniformity, a rigid view of authority, an uncritical support for remaking school curricula in the interest of labor-market imperatives, and a return to the old transmission and acculturation model of teaching. (p. xv)

Despite the myopic efforts of technocratic proponents to subjugate school curricula to the dictates of the labor market, contemporary educational reform would seem to require a different set of sensibilities and an allegiance to spheres of social life beyond the interests of private enterprise and the economic sphere. The progressive movement in education, to which this discussion now turns, emerged during the early decades of this century in reaction to similar restrictive forces in schools to forge a new set of priorities for education.

EXPERIMENTALISM AND EDUCATION:
THE PROGRESSIVE PHILOSOPHY

The progressive education movement in North America is less than a century old, yet during its brief history it has undergone several incarnations, formed allegiances with an assortment of causes, and been variously glorified or condemned by parents, teachers, and the public at large. Emerging in reaction to the authoritarian and antidemocratic nature of traditional schooling in the late nineteenth century, the movement's initial influence reached a peak in the 1920s and 1930s under the leadership of educators such as John Dewey (1859–1952) and William Heard Kilpatrick (1871–1965). Through his writings, Dewey provided the conceptual foundations for progressive education and related the movement to the larger social and political vision of which it was a part. Kilpatrick, perhaps the chief interpreter of Dewey's philosophy, popularized the vision of progressive education and developed a number of its most important practical elements.

Fundamental to Dewey's thinking was the notion of the democratic society as the basis for community life. For Dewey, the term *democracy* implied more than a particular form of government. A truly democratic society fostered an experimental temperament within its citizenry and advocated community-based participatory approaches to decision making. The effectiveness of this type of social arrangement was largely dependent on a well-informed public with skills in critical decision making and community building, hence the need for an educational system which fostered skills in independent thinking and cooperative learning.

Dewey's conception of the educational process contrasted sharply with the traditional, authoritarian, and hierarchical view of learning that dominated the history of schooling up to his time. Underlying traditional education was an atomistic conception of a fixed and predetermined universe which revealed a set of "permanent values" and "static knowledge" that could be transmitted piecemeal to each successive generation. Taking an opposite view, Dewey argued that humans live in an indeterminate world that undergoes constant change and flux. In order to create a sense of meaningfulness and purpose out of this "universe in process," humans did traditionally turn to the fixed authority of various religious and philosophical systems which provided an overriding context for daily life (and the roots of traditional education), but in an age of rapid progress and technological advancement, a reliance on such outdated systems was neither wise nor warranted.

Rather, argued Dewey, it was that vanguard of the modern experience — experimental science — which provided the best tool for understanding the world in which we live. And it was through the disciplined use of the scientific method and the problem-solving process which extended from it that humans could learn to solve most problems and direct the course of future experiences. Dewey's aim was to create a participatory democracy, whereby people from diverse cultural and economic backgrounds could utilize an experimental model of inquiry as the basis for rational planning and decision making. By instilling an experimental temperament in students and helping them to develop basic skills of inquiry, schools fulfilled an important function within such a design.

Kilpatrick (1927) adapted Dewey's problem-solving process (described in Table 2.2) into the project method of teaching and learning. By closely following the experimental model of inquiry outlined by Dewey, the project method gave students the opportunity (with the proper support of their teachers) to plan and direct their own learning experiences and pursue their own research interests. Moreover, it radically transformed the nature of the educational experience for both students and teachers. No longer were students just passive recipients of externally imposed subject matter. Now they were free to be the constructors of their own learning experiences, following the path laid out by the experimental method. Likewise, teachers, released from their traditional role as indoctrinaires, became facilitators of experience and resource persons to whom students could turn for guidance.

Progressive education clearly revolutionized educators' conception of the "cognitive" in education, but it also introduced another form of consciousness to schools. A focus on the individualized learning needs of children naturally led to a greater concern for their emotional and social development. Beginning in the 1960s and 1970s, with the rise of the humanistic movement in psychology, affective goals in education began to gain prominence, especially at the elementary level. The traditional definition of schools as sites for the transmission of knowledge was now expanded to include a concern for the emotional and social lives of children, the culture of the classroom (which was now seen to be a community), and the role of the peer group in socialization. Similarly, curricular activities and programs designed to raise students' self-esteem and build social skills began making inroads into the classroom.

Beyond the original rise of progressive education and its connection to the humanistic movement in psychology, it is important to distinguish between two recent strands of progressivism in education. First, the reemergence of progressive education in the 1960s and early 1970s and its associa-

Table 2.2. The Problem-solving Method and Inquiry Approach in Progressive Education

The problem-solving method and inquiry approach form the methodological foundations of progressive education. Dewey argued that they provide a means by which learning experiences can be grounded within the context of the scientific method and the experimental model of inquiry, thus reducing the role of arbitrary authority in educational decision making and learning.
Dewey (1916/1966) proposed a five step approach to problem solving, which formed the basis for Kilpatrick's project method and the modern day inquiry approach. First, the rise of a *problematic situation* which perplexes the student and/or threatens the student's current understanding of a particular idea or situation. Second, the *defining of the problem* in a clear and overt way. Third, the *search for information* on the problem with the aim of further clarifying the problem and identifying avenues for further exploration. Fourth, the *stating of a potential solution* and/or a tentative hypothesis. Fifth, the *implementation and testing of the solution* or hypothesis and evaluating of its effectiveness in resolving the problematic situation.

The inquiry approach extends from the above methodology and draws on and reinforces a number of important learning and research skills. The Ontario Ministry of Education (1985), for example, have simplified and adapted Dewey's methodology to include the following steps: *exploring, inquiring, predicting, planning and collecting, deciding, communicating, and evaluating.* The inquiry approach teaches children to formulate questions and hypotheses, organize their ideas, collect, interpret, and evaluate evidence, and draw conclusions. Working alone or in small groups, students plan their research agenda, develop inquiry skills, and work toward an understanding of specific theme areas. Teachers assume the role of facilitators of learning. They organize the classroom environment, ensuring that it is conducive to learning and the inquiry process, and help students to develop research skills. Moreover, they serve as resource persons for students.

In addition to the above classroom examples, the problem-solving method has also been applied to various nontraditional teaching settings. It has been adapted to serve special populations of students and used as the basis for managing children's behavior in various therapeutic programs. For example, Rickard and Latel (1974) chronicle the use of the problem-solving method in a therapeutic summer camp program for children with emotional disabilities. Group problem-solving sessions served to give children the opportunity to receive feedback on their behavior from other members of their camper group, particularly in terms of how their behavior contributed to group functioning. When behavior or interpersonal problems arose, the group's counsellors would facilitate a discussion of the problem with the entire camper group. This discussion would aim to clearly identify the problem, brainstorm possible solutions, decide on and implement a solution, and (at a later date) evaluate the effectiveness of the chosen solution. Similarly, Campbell Loughmiller (1965,1974) has used the group problem-solving approach for several decades to treat troubled adolescents in wilderness treatment programs.

tion with the radical open-concept and free school movements. In general, these movements embraced an anti-intellectual stance which, in the view of Stanley Aronowitz and Henry A. Giroux (1993), helped propel the rise of the technocratic call for reform.[3] A second, more moderate strand of progressive education is clearly evident in many schools today under the labels of "child-centered education," "discovery learning," and "the inquiry approach."

Criticisms of the Progressive Perspective

For close to a century now, progressive education has been the movement of choice for parents who seek to nurture the creative and affective side of their children's development, for educational theorists and researchers who view self-actualization as an important goal in learning, and for teachers who value their (relatively) newfound role as facilitators of experience. Recently, however, the merits of progressive education have come into disrepute. Partly this is due to the efforts of technocratic proponents who have successfully mobilized public discontent against the schools. Beyond this, however, may be a growing realization that the experimentalist faith championed by the philosophy of progressivism may not in itself be sufficient to alleviate the global and community challenges we face. The discussion below begins by addressing some of the traditional objections that have been raised against progressive education and moves on to explore a number of contemporary concerns that arise from an environmental vantage point.

The above discussion of progressive education began with a summary overview of some of the educational ideas of John Dewey, but Dewey could be as critical of progressive education as he was of traditional approaches to schooling. In a strict sense, Dewey was a pragmatic philosopher—not a progressive educator—and although the progressive education movement successfully appropriated certain facets of Dewey's thought, it misrepresented other important aspects of his work. The movement's misrepresentation of his ideas on education moved Dewey to sharply censure the child-centered movement and clarify the basic tenets of his pragmatic philosophy of education in *Experience and Education* (1938).

Dewey based his criticisms of progressive education on the view that some progressive schools subscribed to a "dualistic either/or" vision of education and defined themselves negatively, in terms of what they were not—traditional schools. In clarifying this point, he wrote that

> there is always the danger in a new movement that in rejecting the aims and methods of that which it would supplant, it may develop its principles negatively rather than positively and constructively. Then it takes its clew [*sic*] in practice from that which is rejected instead of from the constructive development of its own philosophy . . . all that is required is *not* to do what is done in traditional schools. (pp. 20, 30)

Dewey argued that by rejecting the authoritarian nature of traditional education, it did not follow that progressive schools should reject *all* forms of authority. Nor did a shift from a subject-centered curriculum to a child-centered curriculum justify the abandonment of all forms of systematic knowledge acquisition.

Recounting how some progressive teachers gave little or no direction to the children in their charge for fear of infringing upon their freedom, Dewey related the above argument to the issue of how much freedom children should be allowed in school.[4] In the following passage, Dewey distinguishes between freedom as the product of intelligent, purposeful activity and the illusion of freedom as the equivalent to loss of control:

> It is easy . . . to escape one form of external control only to find oneself in another and more dangerous form of external control. Impulses and desires that are not ordered by intelligence are under the control of accidental circumstances. It may be a loss rather than a gain to escape from the control of another person only to find one's conduct dictated by immediate whim and caprice—that is, at the mercy of impulses into whose formation intelligent judgment has not entered. A person whose conduct is controlled in this way has at most only the illusion of freedom. Actually he is directed by forces over which he has no command. (pp. 64–65)

Dewey's criticisms of the extreme child-centered wing of the progressive education movement reflected the growing disillusionment of many radical educators who sought a more revolutionary role for schools. During the early history of the progressive education movement, social reconstructionist thinkers led by George S. Counts believed that schools should play an active role in transforming society. They seized on Dewey's notion of the school as a *dynamic* rather than a *reflexive* agency and proposed a radical program of action for students. Working in sharp opposition to the technocratic educators of the day, who attempted to make schools better reflect the dictates of the labor market, social reconstructionists sought to utilize schools as vehicles for transforming culture and bringing a lagging society in line with the changing conditions of modern life (for example, see Counts, 1932/1969).

Significantly, many progressives did not share the social reconstructionists' view that the primary function of schools was to serve as a catalyst for social change. Rather, they believed that the expressed needs of the individual child should be the central focus of schools. This set up a dichotomy between the efforts of those progressive educators who argued that the progressive curriculum should be designed around the needs and interests of the child and those who argued that the curriculum should reflect the social and political problems of the day. With the rise in tensions between these two opposing visions in the 1930s and early 1940s came the gradual separation of the reconstructionist wing from the progressive education movement. With this separation, progressive education lost much of the political radicalism and social perceptiveness which defined its early history (temporarily regained in the 1960s and early 1970s) and gradually succumbed to the conservative forces of the day (R. Miller, 1990).

Without a clear social and political agenda from which to argue, progressive educators have in recent years largely lost their prophetic voice and failed to link their educational proposals to the social and political vision of the movement's founders. In many quarters, progressive education presently risks being viewed as no more than a technique—an alternative to the direct instruction approaches advocated by traditional theories of teaching. And in its affirmation of the child as the center of education, progressive education has left itself open for attacks from both the left (for its negation of the reconstructionist elements of its early history) and the right (for its failure to inculcate the knowledge and values of Western culture).

Yet even in the heyday of the movement, progressive education was prone to attacks from both the left and the right, particularly in terms of its tendency toward anti-intellectualism and historical relativism. For emancipatory theorists, progressive education discounted the important role of history in shaping contemporary social movements and struggles (e.g., Indigenous, class, and race struggles). For conservatives, the progressive focus on immediate experience worked against the need to socialize children into the norms and values of traditional Western culture. Writing in the early 1950s, Hilda Neatby (1953) criticized Canadian schools. Her comments reflected the growing concerns of many educational conservatives:

> Progressivists wish to engender democratic attitudes and appreciations of democratic society. They cannot do this effectively by a persistent preoccupation with immediate experience. The pupils must be moved to other times and other societies. They must see human nature in circumstances utterly different from their own if they are to derive any appreciation of permanent values. (p. 150)

Although Neatby's concern for "permanent values" flies in the face of progressive sensibilities, her assessment of the relativistic nature of progressive education addresses the common criticism that progressive education has traditionally failed to engage students in a study of the past. While Dewey himself did not reject the study of history outright, he did argue that we should "reject a knowledge of the past as the *end* of education and thereby only emphasize its importance as a *means*" (1938/1963, p. 23). His point was to capture the utilitarian role of history in shaping the future (see Dewey, 1916/1966, p. 75), but this position was easily misinterpreted by the progressive proponents of the day, who concluded that the study of history as a distinct subject area had no place in the progressive curriculum. As a result, many progressive educators (who were likely also reacting to the influential place accorded to history within traditional education) deemphasized history as an important area for study (Gutek, 1974), a reaction very much in line with the dualistic either/or tendencies of progressive education noted by Dewey and discussed above.

The ahistorical tendencies of progressive education are significant to the focus of this book and serve to underscore the failure of the progressive philosophy to adequately address the ideological roots of the current environmental impasse. As discussed in Chapter 1, our current insights into the environmental crisis are largely rooted in our understanding of the cultural antecedents to this crisis—specific cultural assumptions which have developed in Western cultures since the Enlightenment (and in some cases, earlier). Assumptions such as the notion of "change in nature as always moving forward to cumulative improvement" (Bowers, 1993, p. 95), the glorification of the individual over the social group (held by most progressives, but not by Dewey), and the anthropocentric view of the universe were all held by progressives, who failed to recognize that these were essentially cultural constructions of reality rather than timeless truths. These assumptions embraced the scientific optimism of the day but bred an intolerance toward other types of knowledge, including the authority of tradition, ritual, and myth that is inherent to all cultural groups, but perhaps most notably, Indigenous and Eastern cultures.

Dewey himself attempted to remove culture from the picture. In developing a problem-solving method by which diverse cultural groups could communicate with each other, he ignored and devalued the important role played by cultural stories, rituals, values, and traditions in informing the various beliefs and practices of most of the world's people. That these values and traditions have sustained many cultures for a millennium and successfully rooted their respective cosmologies within the larger context of the earth community is a lesson which should not be so easily dismissed at present.

Yet Dewey was hostile to (and perhaps, by present standards, even prejudiced against) the merits of those societies based on a nonlogical/ analytical plane of consciousness and a nonscientific/nonmodern technological culture (see Dewey, 1938/1963, p. 39). "In violation of his own criticism of dualistic, either–or thinking" writes Ron Miller (1990, p. 105), Dewey argued that schools must either move "backward to the intellectual and moral standards of a pre-scientific age or forward to ever greater utilization of scientific method" (Dewey, 1938/1963, p. 89). Dewey's hostility towards so-called backward cultures reflected his positivistic and experimentalistic faith in the sanctity of the scientific and problem-solving methods for solving contemporary social and political problems. In Dewey's view, only those forms of knowledge which were verifiable through experience and could be proved scientifically had legitimate standing. How complex and sophisticated a society was largely determined its success in solving pressing community problems, and only the modern society possessed the necessary analytical instruments for solving contemporary problems. That these analytical instruments themselves would eventually come to be blamed for contributing to our present environmental predicament (for reasons discussed in Chapter 1) was anticipated by neither Dewey nor any other leading social thinker of his time.

In his critique of Dewey's thought, Bowers (1993) asks four questions of Dewey's philosophy, which he believes seriously limits the potential role that the progressive position can play in effectively responding to the environmental crisis. Bowers asks:

> What is the form of culture that would emerge if Dewey's epistemological orientation could be made the basis of everyday life? Would Dewey's "method of intelligence" allow for taking seriously the ecologically sustainable practices of traditional cultural groups? Is there any basis in Dewey's dynamic model for forms of moral authority that would frame human actions in terms of self-limitation for the sake of future generations of the biotic community, and how would these forms of moral authority be symbolically grounded? My own judgment is that when the answer to the first question is adequately worked out, the limitations of Dewey's thinking will become clearer. (pp. 99–100)

In light of this discussion, it would be a mistake to assume that the progressive position forwards the most viable plan for educational reform simply because of its historical reputation as a leading edge philosophy. As Bowers (1993, p. 88) warns, "ideologies previously viewed as progressive may now represent reactionary positions," in light of the environmental challenges we currently face. The philosophical foundations of progressive education were laid down well before the inability of the planet to support unlimited economic expansion was widely understood. John Dewey and other progressive proponents supported (in some cases, even glorified) this expansion and the technological development that went along with it, and the term *progressive* was itself partly derived from a faith in the sanctity of economic and technological progress to increase quality of life and solve pressing community problems. Only in recent decades has this technological optimism been seriously called into question by environmental proponents who recognize the dangerous assumptions inherent to such thinking.

Keeping these comments in mind, we should not be surprised to find that the ideological underpinnings of progressivism (including the reconstructionist wing of the movement) reflect a commitment to "social progress" and "economic growth" which is largely consistent with the idea of progress forwarded by proponents of the technocratic philosophy. Although progressives would like to see a more rigorous commitment to environmental protection in the United States and Canada (as well as a more equitable distribution of national wealth in these countries), and although progressives support an interventionist role for government in both regards, their failure to put forward an incisive critique of the materialistic and anthropocentric foundations of the industrialized world, coupled with their commitment to a monolithic approach to problem-solving, means that their efforts aimed at democratic and cultural renewal are likely to play no more than a cursory role in addressing the ideological roots of the current environmental impasse.

Almost a century has passed since the progressive philosophy first ushered in and articulated the promise of a rapidly industrializing society. Today, however, the merits of this optimism are being challenged by a number of other social movements. Included among these movements is the holistic philosophy which forwards its own proposals for educational reform. We turn to these in the following discussion.

SPIRITUALITY AND EDUCATION: THE HOLISTIC PHILOSOPHY

The term *holistic* has been used in a variety of ways by different people in education. Its most conservative meaning refers to a system of education or curriculum that crosses two or more subject boundaries — for example, using English literature as the vehicle for teaching European history.

Sometimes the term has been used to refer to the whole language approach to the teaching of reading and writing. Often the term has been confused with the progressive position reviewed above. In reality, none of the above caricatures provides an adequate basis for understanding the philosophical underpinnings of the holistic philosophy; rather, each offers only a superficial view of the ideological foundations which underlie the holistic vision for education. In contrast to the single-minded approach to problem-solving advocated by the progressive position, for example, holistic proponents forward a multifaceted approach to "knowing" which incorporates a variety of types of consciousness (e.g., intuitive, kinesthetic, and spiritual consciousness). Similarly, the holistic position counters Dewey's silence on the culture issue by directly addressing the role of myth, story, and tradition in shaping identity and sustaining a sense of meaningfulness and purpose across the life span.

The holistic vision for education arises within the context of the perennial philosophy which forwards an ecological view of the world. From the holistic perspective, all phenomena in nature are seen to be interconnected within an interdependent universe. This interdependency is based on a reciprocity within and between the natural, physical, and cultural worlds which permeate our lives and the entire biotic community. Recent advances in quantum physics and the rise of the science of ecology tend to support the holistic position that the connections which bind objects and phenomena together are just as important as the objects and phenomena themselves. Arising out of an ecological conception of the world, the holistic perspective emerges in sharp contrast to the atomistic notion of a disconnected, fragmented world which was critiqued in Chapter 1. As John P. Miller (1988) writes in his seminal work on holistic education:

> In atomism the universe is viewed as a collection of atoms; in [progressivism] it is seen as an ongoing process; in holism it is perceived as harmonious and interconnected. Holism acknowledges the individual part and that things are in process; however, there is a fundamental unity underlying the process and connecting the parts . . . the emphasis is on the *relations* between the whole and the part. (p. 18)

A focus on connections has led holistic educators to value a wide variety of approaches to "knowing" which complement the logical–analytic forms of knowledge traditionally legitimated in schools. These include *intuitive* thought processes, which entail direct and immediate contact with knowledge, a cognitive process unmediated by rational consideration or analysis, which arises most often during moments of intense creative activity or when the body is at rest, but the mind alert; *metaphorical* thought processes, which entail cognitive leaps in thought which bridge by analogy two seemingly unrelated phenomena and thus uncover new relationships and patterns; and *narrative* modes of thought in which the temporal basis of life is given voice and sequences of events are reconstructed to capture meaning.

The notion of *spirituality* is central to the holistic philosophy. Here the term does not imply any particular religious dogma or otherworldly tradition; rather, it entails our continuous search for meaningfulness and purpose in the world. How we make sense of the world and the ideological frameworks and "guiding metaphors" that inform human practices and cultural beliefs are all inherent elements of the holistic notion of spiritual consciousness. So too is the young child's intuitive understanding of the way the world works and the scientist's reliance on the experimental method as a tool of analysis. Both the child and scientist find meaning in a particular way of understanding and interpreting the world around them.

Holistic proponents regard spirituality to be both personally and culturally constructed and inwardly and outwardly directed. As individuals, we are constantly engaged in a search for meaningfulness and purpose throughout our lives (a search which likely becomes more intense as we face new challenges and embark on new experiences), but our sense of meaningfulness and purpose is also informed by various cultural factors, including our national and racial identities, religious affiliations, and the beliefs and traditions of significant others, our families, and communities. The search for meaningfulness and purpose can be an intensely personal, even private, journey, or find expression through communion with others in celebration, achievement, and other shared experiences.

The holistic curriculum addresses the child's search for meaningfulness and purpose in the natural world and the physical and cultural worlds which surround the child. Holistic educators regard this search to be both inwardly directed by the child and outwardly directed by the teacher and curriculum. By paying critical attention to the child's inner motivations and time-critical stages of growth, holistic educators argue that they are able to effectively respond to children's needs at various stages of development. In this way, writes Ron Miller (1992, p. 20), the holistic philosophy "starts with a profound respect for the growing human being and seeks to provide a learning environment" that is congruent with and responsive to the developmental tasks of successive stages of development.

The holistic education movement comprises a number of distinct educational traditions which unite around the core beliefs and principles outlined above. Within many models of holistic education, artistic endeavors—including the visual arts, handicrafts, music, poetry, movement, dance, drama, and storytelling—are featured prominently and may even form the basis of the curriculum. Other holistic models integrate nonanalytical forms of cognition into the learning process. Within these traditions, guided visualization activities (see Table 2.3) and narrative/metaphorical instructional strategies are used alongside other more traditional approaches to teaching. Still other holistic traditions emphasize community connections—students learn about the ecological, cultural, and economic infrastructure of their local communities and the different professional roles which contribute to its daily functioning. Within such programs, students may participate in apprenticeship-style programs or become involved with social action projects designed to contribute to the overall improvement of the community.

Perhaps the two most well-known traditions within the holistic philosophy are the Montessori and Waldorf school movements. Each of these traditions finds its roots within a detailed interpretive account of development in childhood related to the child's emerging cosmology of the world. In each tradition a series of time-critical stages finds expression via the child's inner motivations and strivings, which provide the context for the methodology and curricular foundations of each level of the child's education. Although in many respects juxtaposed in emphasis and design (Cohn,

Table 2.3. Visualization Activities in Holistic Education

Guided visualization journeys are used on occasion by some holistic educators to heighten the receptive powers of the intuitive process by evoking flights of fantasy within a structured atmosphere of relaxation and security. Depending on the specific circumstances in which the journey is conducted, the optimal setup might be as follows: The students lie on the floor (or alternatively sit at a desk, arms folded, heads down, and eyes closed). The lights are turned off or down low and relaxing instrumental music plays in the background. The leader speaks softly and reassuringly, spacing her instructions by several seconds.

A typical visualization journey can be designed using the following four components:

1. *Tension and Relaxation Exercises* (2–4 minutes) focus attention and energy on specific parts of the body in an attempt to set a comfortable rhythm for the journey, relax the participants, and heighten sensory awareness. Typically, the leader begins at one end of the body, often focusing first on the toes, then on the heels and so on until each part of the body has received attention. For example, "Push the weight of your heels against the floor. Now relax...Make a tight fist with your hands. And relax."

2. *The Journey* (4–7 minutes) begins when the learners are slowly "lifted" from their bodies and travel to a distant place. They imagine looking down at themselves as they are lifted higher and higher. The leader points out specific sensations along the way, such as the gentle touch of the clouds across the face, or the change in temperature at different altitudes

3. *The Visit* (5–10 minutes) establishes the purpose for the journey and is often the source of the learner's greatest satisfaction. The visit is most effective when the focus is on a single person or item, such as the exchange of ideas between the learner and another individual or the manipulation of an object of inquiry. In some cases, who or what each student visits can be left up to the learner herself, but if the aim of the visualization is to introduce specific subject material, the leader may prefer to use a more directed approach. As this is the focal point of the journey, considerable attention is usually given to planning this component

4. *The Journey Home* (3–5 minutes) carefully retraces the original journey in terms of sights, touches, and other nuances, culminating in the return to the body. The leader quietly announces the end of the journey and allows time for the learners to "awaken" at their own pace.

Many holistic educators believe that a guided journey which uses the above structure can contribute a richness in variety and possibility to the language arts, geography, history, and other subject areas. Other types of visualization activities are more appropriately used in conjunction with mathematics and science. It's all a matter of to what places the leader takes the learners and whom (or what) they meet there. The students may become archaeologists in search of the artifacts of a distant civilization, or they may envision themselves in the front lines beside Paul Baumer in *All Quiet on the Western Front*. In each case, the journey's contribution to the intuitive mode is the high degree to which it evokes strong visual imagery and recreates a sense of high drama or personal intimacy.

1990), the Montessori and Waldorf approaches are united, as are most other traditions within holistic education, in the attention to detail given to understanding the child from a developmental perspective and increasingly within the context of an ecological view of the world.

Criticisms of the Holistic Perspective

In sharp contrast to the technocratic and progressive philosophies reviewed earlier, the holistic philosophy would seem to forward an ecologically sensitive view of the educational process. Such a view emerges within an ecological conception of the world that places the human within the larger context of the earth community and provides the underlying basis for the methodology and subject matter of holistic education. Yet despite its ecological roots, the holistic philosophy is not wholly immune from criticisms that arise from an environmental vantage point. The criticisms that can be brought against holistic education are, however, less substantive in nature than those aimed at technocratic and progressive education, and they reflect "areas for improvement" in light of our understanding of the cultural dimensions of the ecological crisis. Whereas the ideological foundations of technocratic and progressive education reveal severe limitations in this regard, the discussion above would seem to indicate that the holistic position shows some promise in addressing the cultural dimensions of the ecological crisis. But unless these kernels of reform can be captured and nurtured, the holistic position risks losing its privileged status as an ecologically sensitive philosophy of education. Three specific criticisms of the holistic education movement need to be examined in this regard. First, the failure of the holistic movement to distance itself from the ecologically problematic strands of radical educational reform; second, the failure of many holistic educators to recognize the anthropocentric foundations (and thus limitations) of the humanistic and transpersonal strands in holistic education; and finally, the need for holistic education to better address issues of personal and social justice.

The first criticism concerns problems with the scope of holistic education. A variety of educational traditions fall under the label of holistic education and a central concern for a number of holistic theorists is to explore the relationships between these traditions and uncover the basic principles and beliefs which unite these traditions under the title of "holistic" (the journal *Holistic Education Review* has been infinitely helpful in this regard). Although most holistic educators would concur with Edward T. Clark's (1991) statement that diversity within holistic education is valuable and should be defended, the situation becomes problematic when the root assumptions of specific traditions within holistic education come into direct conflict with one another. This can be clearly seen in the example of the liberationist movement in education, which has been interpreted by some holistic educators to fall under the auspices of the holistic education label, particularly in recent surveys of holistic education.

In contrast to the ideological foundations of holistic education reviewed above, liberationist theorists, led perhaps by the vision of A. S. Neill, have argued vehemently against the role of teacher authority in education and called for the dismantling of formal schooling (and the introduction of "open" or "free" schools) and the liberation of the child. Although some elements of the liberationist argument are helpful in *critiquing* the oppressive aspects of traditional approaches to education, many of the reform proposals forwarded by liberationists that aim to address this oppression are fundamentally juxtaposed against both an ecologically sensitive approach to education and the notion of holistic education as reviewed in this chapter. Rather than representing divergent but complementary reinterpretations of the same basic set of assumptions (or "first principles"), holistic education and the liberationist tradition are viewed here to be virtually irreconcilable.

The liberationist tradition in education is ecologically problematic because it glorifies the value of the individual over the social group and community and undercuts the important role of schools as socializing institutions and potential sites for the cultural transmission of ecologically sensitive values. (There are also problems with the child liberationist strand within this tradition, which are addressed in Chapter 5.) More specifically, the liberationist position posits individual freedom and autonomy as a basic goal of education, but it attaches little or no importance to the value of the larger community, except as a site where individual freedom can be secured and regulated (this was the function of self-government in A. S. Neill's *Summerhill* school). Restriction of freedom and behavior is a central point of contention for liberationists, but it is precisely such restrictions which are made necessary by the deepening environmental impasse. In contrast to Alexander Solzhenitsyn's ecological redefinition of freedom as the "restriction of the self for the sake of others" (1974, p. 136), liberationist theorists argue for a notion of freedom and individuality which is fundamentally atomistic and self-serving in nature and largely unaccountable to the needs of the wider earth community.

Within the context of the present work, the liberationist tradition in education is not seen to fall within the domain of holistic education. Rather, such a tradition is viewed to be a radical extension of the extreme child-centered movement in progressive education (but not of Dewey's thought). Including the liberationist tradition under the veil of holistic education would unnecessarily make the holistic position as ecologically problematic as the progressive and technocratic positions reviewed earlier and serve only to direct attention away from those elements of holistic education which are ecologically responsible. Moreover, the central tenets of the liberationist position are in direct conflict with the ideological foundations of many other traditions within holistic education. The central role played by community in holistic education, for example, is largely discounted by the liberationist movement, as is the facilitative role of the teacher. (The Waldorf notion that the young child "lives through" the significant adults in her life would, for example, be completely foreign to liberationists, but not to other traditions within holistic education.) Perhaps the liberationist tradition is attractive to some holistic educators because of its radical nature, but this is to confuse a "progressive" position of the past with what amounts to a reactionary (and even dangerous) position of the present.

Once the central tenets of the liberationist position are fully clarified, it should not be difficult to see that this tradition and holistic education share very little in common. There is, however, another somewhat more significant line of thought running through holistic discourse that poses its own ecological problems. This is the tendency for some holistic educators to emphasize the interior, spiritual life of the individual over the more substantial connections which can be forged between individuals and the wider earth community. Insofar as holistic education is simply seen to provide a path to personal empowerment, individual fulfillment, and self-actualization, the cultural dimensions of the ecological crisis are likely to remain ignored.

The glorification of the individual within certain humanistic and transpersonal strands of holistic education reveals a degree of anthropocentricism which matches that of the technocratic, progressive, and liberationist philosophies. Many contemplative practices which have had a long, rich history within the holistic movement are presently being challenged by the ecological crisis to account for the *entire* earth community within their conceptions of human fulfillment and empowerment. The challenge to these traditions is to equate human development and actualization with what Thomas Berry (1988, p. 82) terms "the enhancement of life for the entire planetary community," rather than narrowly defining "individual human experience" as the "fountain of social progress" (Miller, R., 1991b, p. 49). Just as human health needs to be tied to the well-being of the earth community, so too our experience of the sacred needs to be rooted within a biocentric cosmology rather than an anthropocentric one.

Perhaps the greatest challenge facing the holistic movement at present does not arise (directly) from the vantage point of the ecological crisis, but rather from a failure to address seriously issues of personal and social justice, and by extension, the role of violence in the lives of children (which is a focus of Chapter 5). To the same degree that most critical and emancipatory theorists, such as Paulo Freire and Henry Giroux, have failed to take account of the spiritual realm in human consciousness and virtually ignored the ecological crisis (Bowers, 1993), the holistic philosophy has been noticeably silent on issues related to the "ethical realm" of human existence. As Ron Miller (1991a) argues:

> Many holistic thinkers have addressed the need for personal development, but they have largely neglected important cultural and ideological questions. On the other hand, most critical theorists seem to lack an appreciation for the interior life and the spiritual/ecological context of human existence. (pp. 2–3)

One of the explanations for the above silence may be that many holistic educators do not differentiate between the ethical and spiritual realms; rather, values and ethics are seen to emerge within a spiritual context. While this may not be problematic in itself, it does limit the role that holistic education can play in responding effectively to situations of extreme suffering and injustice which seem devoid of meaning and purpose and beyond (spiritual) apprehension. As argued in Hutchison (1991):

> It does not come easy for the individual who chooses to engage the ethical dimension, since one is compelled not only to acknowledge but also to account for and deeply involve oneself in the tragic realities of the lives of so many of the world's peoples. One must choose (and in the face of pain and suffering, keep choosing) as his or her palette the totality of human experiences no matter how actualizing or wicked they may be, for these cannot remain ignored or unaccounted for within a holistic model of humankind. (p. 14)

Although the spiritual realm can "serve as a buffer of reassurance" in the face of suffering and injustice and "restore an element of hope to our apprehension of the world" (Hutchison, 1991, p. 16), this response alone is not sufficient to counter the forces of oppression, suffering, and injustice which exist throughout the world. Such action requires a concerted effort, a clear moral commitment, risk, struggle, and ideological resistance — actions that emerge, at least in part, from an ethical realm of consciousness. Articulating just what role educators should play in this struggle for justice and peace remains one of the most pressing obligations of the holistic philosophy,[5] for as Purpel and Miller (1991) argue, "a genuinely *holistic* educational theory — a holism that is truly whole — must draw upon a well-defined human development/spiritual orientation *as well as* a critical social and political perspective" (p. 34).

TOWARD A NEW VISION OF EDUCATION

From the perspective of educational reform, the discussion in this chapter would seem to indicate that the holistic philosophy affords the most promise for effectively dealing with the environmental crisis that currently confronts us. At the level of ideology, neither the technocratic philosophy nor the progressive philosophy adequately addresses the fragile state of the planet's life systems or the role of the human within the larger context of the earth community. Rather, it has been argued that the technocratic philosophy is itself a symptom of the problem and the progressive philosophy fails to address the cultural roots of the crisis. Despite its infancy as a model for education, and present lack of focus on issues of personal and social justice, the holistic philosophy is judged to provide the best educational context for dealing with the environmental challenges we presently face.

This is not the end of the story, however. As mentioned above, such a conclusion is based solely on an assessment of the *ideological* merits of each of the three philosophies. At the level of *practice*, it is possible (perhaps even likely) that each philosophy (and others) can make an important contribution to a new vision for education. In reference to Dewey's criticisms of the dualistic either/or tendencies of progressive education discussed earlier, two questions can genuinely be asked: Is it necessary to reject the unique and potentially valuable elements of all other philosophies in favor of a total commitment to any one approach to education? Can educators not play out essential elements of all three philosophical positions reviewed above in their daily activities as teachers?

This chapter closes by suggesting an alternative to the adversarial arrangement of the technocratic, progressive, and holistic philosophies which may provide a satisfactory answer to these questions. It is possible to regard each of the philosophical positions reviewed in this chapter as more *inclusive* than the one that precedes it in the discussion above. In this sense the progressive philosophy can be seen to be more inclusive than the technocratic position and the holistic philosophy can be viewed as being more inclusive than the progressive position. Within such a design, each successive philosophy encompasses and expands upon, but does not supersede, the valuable elements of the more restricted positions.

For example, each philosophy subscribes to a broader conception of consciousness and "ways of knowing" than the one preceding it. For each philosophy, a wider breadth of consciousness is deemed to be within the mandate of schools or of legitimate concern to educators. The technocratic philosophy values forms of knowledge which have a strong *cognitive* base and are rooted within traditional intellectual disciplines. In practice, this translates into a focus on mastery learning, technical skills, and standard-ized forms of testing. The progressive position expands upon this somewhat limited view of the cognitive to also include that which can be verified through experience and the experimental method. And just as important, through its focus on the individual needs of the child, the progressive philos-ophy incorporates the *affective* realm of consciousness into the educational experience by way of activities which promote the social growth of students and the healthy development of self-concept. Finally, the holistic philoso-phy incorporates intuitive and metaphorical modes of knowing into the above logical/analytic conception of the cognitive and introduces a *spiritual* dimension to the educational experience which addresses the child's search for meaningfulness and purpose in the world.

In a manner similar to the above, John P. Miller and his associates (1990) write that each successive position can be seen to be more inclusive than the one prior to it as "we move from the more restrictive scope of an atomistic perspective to a more inclusive view that witnesses the connec-tions between ourselves and many levels of experience and knowledge" (p. 6). Within this context, the progressive paradigm encompasses (but again does not supersede) the technocratic focus on basic literacy, technique, and systematic knowledge acquisition and applies such components to the task of problem-solving. Holistic education, in turn, embraces the inquiry and problem-solving approaches popularized by progressive education, but uti-lizes them alongside other complementary strategies for learning and within an overall curricular framework for education.

An example of how the above inclusionary approach can work in classrooms on a day-to-day basis might be helpful. In her celebrated book *In the Middle: Writing, Reading, and Learning with Adolescents* (1987), Nancie Atwell reflects on her experiences working with upper elementary school students and outlines her language arts program for a whole lan-guage approach to the teaching of reading and writing. Atwell's approach incorporates many traditional elements of a whole language program, in-cluding "editing conferences" and "sharing circles," but significantly, it also regularly involves small groups of students in "mini-lessons" designed to teach and reinforce basic skills in grammar, punctuation, spelling, and other writing skills. While Atwell's language arts program firmly rests within the traditions of progressive and holistic education, it also does not shy away from the technocratic call for systematic instruction in the basics.

The point we may take from the above example is that a truly holistic approach to teaching and learning does not relinquish the technocratic focus on basic skills, nor does it ignore the progressive educator's concern for the social development of each child. Rather, significant aspects of both the technocratic and progressive philosophies are integrated into a holistic vision for education. The technocratic call for systematic instructional approaches reminds holistic educators that under certain circumstances, an atomistic, teacher-directed instructional approach may be required. So too there are many valuable resources within the progressive tradition which address the social and emotional needs of children (e.g., Canfield and Wells, 1976). While it is argued that the philosophical foundations of holistic education should provide the overriding context for a new vision of education, it is emphasized that valuable practical elements from all three philosophical positions reviewed in this chapter can make important contributions to educational practice. Yet what is most required is a coherent vision and curriculum framework for holistic education that can best help us resolve the environmental and other challenges we presently face.

CHAPTER 3

Myth and Functionality
in the Cultural Construction
of Childhood

When focusing attention upon childhood as the most specific biological pecu-
liarity in human life history, we find ourselves at an intersection of biological
and cultural evolution, with perspectives leading both into the past and to-
ward the future.
            —Edith Cobb, *The Ecology of Imagination in Childhood* (1977)

Chapter 2 reviewed and critiqued the ideological foundations of three contemporary philosophies of education. It was argued that proponents for
each subscribe to different views of the educational process and forward
competing agendas for school reform. The ideological foundations which
underlie the technocratic, progressive, and holistic visions for education are
not, however, limited to a specific vision of curriculum, instructional design, and educational goals. Each of these perspectives also forwards a
unique and contrasting conception of childhood — a conception which in all
three cases serves to substantiate and underscore the central ideology which
informs each tradition.

As emphasized in Chapter 2, technocratic proponents forward an economic view of the educational process that is largely driven by the human
resources needs of a future postindustrial society. Implicit to this view is the
notion that children are economic resources who make (care of their parents) investments in their "human capital" (i.e., economic potential) by
using a cost-benefit approach to calculate the economic rates of return
for various training and educational investment opportunities (DeYoung,
1989). Within such a conception, differences between children and adults
(in terms of cognitive functioning and ways of seeing the world) are judged
to be largely minimal, since both the adult and "technocratic child" are

actively involved in upgrading and maximizing their knowledge, skills, and employment potential.

In contrast to the above economic view of the child, the progressive child is regarded to be an active participant in formulating and reformulating the world around her. By using the inquiry method as a "model of reflective intelligence" for engaging the world, the child is able to secure her goals and learn to problem-solve effectively. The results of her explorations lead to a further restatement of her aims, and new experiences are then subjected to the method of inquiry. Evelina Orteza y Miranda's (1982) statement below reflects this view. She writes that the progressive child

> is an agent who acts and interacts with the environment . . . he is an intimate participant in the activities of the world . . . these activities, guided by ideas or previous experiences, bring about relationships or connections between the child and his environment. Such results may be termed outcomes of inquiry or knowledge. The knowledge he now possesses the child employs to solve problems of whatever kind, to explore further into his environment, the results of which could lead to the modification of the environment intended to secure desirable social ends . . . [the progressive] child is an active creator of the world which he inhabits. And that which he creates he also subjects to further inquiry, [thus] promoting more knowledge, connections with the world. This knowledge, in turn, increases his consciousness of his control over the conduct of inquiry. His intelligent employment of it could mean that the direction and outcomes of future experiences are secured. (pp. 35–36)

Implicit to the above conception of childhood is the child's manipulation of the outside world and the separation of "knower" from "known." Development in childhood entails the child's gradual mastery of the surrounding physical and symbolic worlds through the disciplined use of rational intelligence. In contrast to this,[1] the "holistic child" is seen to be embedded in the world and it is a *reciprocity* between child and world that moves development to new levels. Jules Michelet (1846/1973), the great French historian, expresses perhaps the cardinal principle of the holistic vision of childhood when he writes that children

> compare and connect very willingly, but they seldom divide or analyze. Not only does every kind of division trouble their minds, but it pains them and seems to dismember reality. They do not like dissecting life, and everything seems to them to have life. All things, whatever they may be, are for them organic beings which they are very careful not to alter in the slightest way. They draw back the moment it is necessary to disturb by analysis anything that shows the least appearance of vital harmony . . . Not only do they not divide, but as soon as they find anything divided or partial, they either neglect it or mentally reconstitute this whole with a rapidity of imagination that could not

be expected from their natural slowness . . . Their mutual understanding is due to one thing—their common sympathy for nature and life, which causes them to delight only in a unity that lives. (pp. 138–140)

From the above passages it seems clear that what constitutes childhood is itself contested within the technocratic, progressive, and holistic philosophies of education. Beyond this limited focus, however, may be wider cultural discrepancies in the "idea of the child" held by parents, developmental psychologists, and past/present generations of various cultures. Pinpointing the roots of these discrepancies is the focus of the present chapter. The notion that childhood is a static entity which has existed in its present manifestation from time immortal is challenged, as is the idea that there is a "true" nature of childhood which is awaiting discovery. By exploring the multifaceted dimensions of what might be termed *the cultural construction of childhood*, this chapter seeks to provide the conceptual basis and launching point for a new story of development in middle childhood (Chapter 4) that addresses the role of the child in the recovery of sustainable relations with the natural world.

Implicit to the argument of this chapter are a number of general principles which were originally forwarded by Allison James and Alan Prout (1990). The first of these, as stated above, is that *"childhood is understood as a social construction . . . [it] is neither a natural nor universal feature of human groups but appears as a specific structural and cultural component of many societies"* (pp. 8–9, emphasis added). A distinction is made here between genetic coding, which is the biological basis of our existence, and cultural coding, which comprises all of the ways and means by which we have given meaning to our existence across time and place (e.g., our norms, values, cultural stories, and traditions) and also the technological products and artifacts of this existence (Berry, 1988). Development in childhood has both biological and cultural roots. Among other achievements, children are genetically mandated in early childhood to learn how to walk and talk. Mastery of these skills allows the child to apprehend and transform the physical and symbolic universe which surrounds her, which is the basis of cultural life. The flip side of this process is that following a biologically mandated period of early childhood (in which language and mobility skills are acquired) childhood is henceforth itself largely an artifact of human construction. (Two important exceptions to this position will be identified in Chapter 5.)

A second principle is that *"childhood is a variable of social analysis. It can never be entirely divorced from other variables such as class, gender, or ethnicity."* It is argued that the cultural construction of childhood cannot be fully understood without reference to a number of implicit factors which

inform our conceptions of childhood. These include the social and historical context, the idea and role of the child in society, child rearing approaches and socialization subpatterns, and theories of development. Each
of these factors is addressed below. Third, *"children's social relationships
and cultures are worthy of study in their own right, independent of the
perspective and concerns of adults."* The culture of childhood includes all
that is not determined by adults. Holistic theorists in particular have sought
to understand more fully the inner life of the child, as well as the pivotal
role played by peer culture and "place-making" in the lives of children. Each
is briefly explored below. Fourth, *"children are and must be seen as active
in the construction and determination of their own social lives, the lives of
those around them and of the societies in which they live. Children are not
just the passive subjects of social structures and processes."* The notion
of reciprocity in the cultural construction of childhood and the cultural
construction of the world is critical here. Just as the world is a constructor
of the child, so too the child is a constructor of the world. Lewis Thomas's
hypothesis (1983) that the evolution of a latent disposition for speech in the
human species coupled with children's play behavior in groups played a key
role in the origins of language holds true here, but perhaps most important,
given the argument of this book, is the role that the "natural" aptitudes of
children can presently play in helping the human species to recover a sense
of connectedness to the natural world. Finally, it is argued that *"to proclaim
a new paradigm of childhood sociology is also to engage in and respond to
the process of reconstructing childhood in society."* Despite the implicit
relativism which a constructivist thesis (such as is forwarded here) implies,
no suggestion is made that we should forgo attempts to build a better life
for children at present. Rather, an obligation to better meet the needs of
children still remains. Toward the end of this chapter (and again in Chapter
5) the concept of *functionality* is utilized as a way of judging the effectiveness of specific constructions of childhood in meeting the physical and
psychosocial needs of children and further indicating the role or place of the
child in the recovery of sustainable relations with the natural world.

SOME MYTHIC ASPECTS OF CONTEMPORARY
DEVELOPMENTAL THEORY

Although certain fundamental aspects of childhood are clearly universal
(e.g., children are born small and grow big), it seems clear that child psychologists have "invented" different children through the ages. For the most
part, the major twentieth century traditions within developmental psychology do not have as their fundamental aim the elucidation of a single, spe-

cific aspect of development in childhood (although this is a pattern in recent psychological research). Instead, each has attempted to build an overriding and all-encompassing context for understanding the nature of the child and the constituent elements of development. Furthermore, most give conflicting interpretations of what those constituent elements might be. As William Kessen (1983) writes (somewhat satirically):

> Sigmund Freud observed Anna and found wish fulfillment, John Watson observed Billy and found unconditioned responses, Jean Piaget observed Jacqueline and found adaptive assimilation, B. F. Skinner observed Debra and found a baby in a box . . . John Locke was a bachelor and Jean-Jacques Rousseau sent his five children to the Paris foundling home as soon as they were born, yet they were able to provide surefooted categorical descriptions of another two kinds of children. (p. 28)

Like all constructions of the world, developmental psychology — and by extension, all scientific traditions — arise from and are embedded within a specific sociocultural and historical context. This context informs the underlying ideological suppositions of the discipline and provides a basic framework for interpreting research data. Valsiner (1987) describes the underlying suppositions of developmental theorists as "cognitive folk models" (p. 40) which serve to give meaning to what is apprehended by the researchers. Valsiner argues that in developmental psychology, as in other scientific traditions,

> data are never theory-free or "objective" in themselves, but constitute results of the investigator's social construction process. Traditionally the data have been talked about in psychology as the ultimate proof of the objectivity of theories. This position itself is based on some basic hidden assumptions in the scientists' culture, as it assumes the independence of the object of investigation from the investigator. (pp. 13–14)

Among the most conspicuous of the assumptions underlying developmental psychology is the notion of progressive and incremental change in childhood. That "development proceeds through sequential, ordered, [and] increasingly complex stages" (Johnson, 1991, p. 18) is inherent to most theories of development and implies that the child moves from an immature state of incompleteness in infancy into a mature state of completeness in adulthood. In many mainstream theories, an important (and often unscrutinized) consequence to this habit of thought is an ideological orientation which implicitly values "adult reality" over "child reality" as the normative point of reference for studying children. Johnson underscores the point in this way:

If the ultimate criterion for judging the objective truth and thus the validity of any mental, moral, religious, or aesthetic experience is its place on the cognitive hierarchy, then childhood experience is already subtly denigrated. (p. 18)

This "subtle denigration" of childhood experience operates in a colonizing fashion, according to Baker and Freebody (1989), as well-meaning developmental psychologists, parents, teachers, and other adults attend to, define, evaluate, and contextualize childhood experience solely in terms of those adult capacities to which children do not yet have recourse:

Most common sense conceptions of childhood and psychological and sociological theories of development posit a particular arrival point in adulthood. There is evident in all such accounts a version of the mature, properly functioning adult, towards which state children progress under the guidance and supervision of adults . . . Data collected within these theoretical frameworks, therefore, tend to document and itemize children's incompetencies or precompetencies in terms of the final desired state . . . It is in these senses that both common sense conceptions and scientific accounts of childhood operate in a colonizing fashion. The attention of the colonists is focused on those aspects of indigenous activity and culture which, in comparison with their own, can be defined as different and inferior . . . This attention arises not necessarily from a lack of interest in the culture of the indigenes—some aspects of it might be found amusing, noble, or clever—but from the assumption of the superior competence and culture of the colonizing group. (p. 25)

In the passage below, Kohlberg and Mayer (1978) make it clear that they subscribe to the view which the above authors elucidate. They argue that the fundamental aim of development in childhood

is the eventual attainment of a higher level or stage of development in adulthood, not merely the healthy functioning of the child at the present level . . . A more developed psychological state is more valuable or adequate than a less developed state. (p. 62)

It is perhaps unfortunate that while our story of childhood has never been more precise and rich in detail than it is at present, it is in certain respects also an impoverished one, in that the potentially unique qualities of childhood risk remaining uncharted within mainstream developmental theory. In the present age, the adult interpreter of the child is the developmental psychologist whose tales generally have as their starting point not the capacities and qualities of experience *unique* to childhood, but the adult faculties which the child lacks. In the same way that the psychologist's notions of the healthy personality have in the past been shaped by his understanding of the unhealthy one, many developmental theorists have learned to account for the child's growth almost solely in terms of the adult capacities she has not yet acquired or acquired in only a very limited way. The child's unique experience of the world is at best mediated through the adult's conception of reality, at worst relegated to insignificance.

The notion that change in childhood is inherently progressive and incremental in nature is implicit to most models of childhood and underscores the pivotal role played by *myth* in developmental psychology. Here the term myth does not (necessarily) imply a negative connotation; rather, myth is essential if we are to be able to formulate a "total" (i.e., complete) view of the child (or any other phenomenon). Myth refers to those implicit aspects of our cultural construction of childhood which underlie, broaden, connect, contextualize, and fill in the missing pieces of our notions of childhood. The examples below highlight how the social and historical context originally shaped (or potentially shaped) the mythic aspects of two of the leading twentieth century traditions in developmental psychology.

The Psychoanalytic Model of Childhood

In 1896, Sigmund Freud (1856–1939) delivered a paper to the Vienna Society for Psychiatry and Neurology ("The Aetiology of Hysteria") in which he argued that the causes of psychological illness (specifically hysteria) could invariably be traced to sexual trauma in early childhood. The paper, Freud's first major public address to his peers, was based on his analytic treatment of 18 patients who reported being sexually abused as young children. His hypothesis that psychological illness in adulthood could be traced to sexual trauma in early childhood came to be known as the "seduction theory." Reaction to Freud's conclusions was not kind. Freud was advised never to publish the paper (advice he did not take), for fear his career would be ruined. Reference to the paper's presentation in the conference proceedings was terse and contained no summary of Freud's findings (Masson, 1984). In the year following this, perhaps as a result of pressure from respected colleagues, Freud wrote to his friend and chief confidant, Wilhelm Fliess, that he had abandoned his seduction hypothesis and now attributed accounts of sexual abuse in early childhood to patients' fantasies and the projection of young children's own unconscious infantile sexual desires onto adults. Accounts of sexual violation in early childhood were not "real," Freud argued in sharp contrast to his earlier position, but were reflections of the fantasy worlds of children. Freud constructed a complex theoretical design, mythic in origins (the "drive theory"), to account for these fantasies.

Although Freud attributed his abandonment of the seduction theory to new theoretical understandings and clinical findings, it also seems plausible

that the social and historical context of the day *may* have been a contributing factor in Freud's suppression of the seduction theory and the consequent
development of the mythic roots of the psychoanalytic model of childhood.
In revealing his potentially scandalous findings in 1896, Freud directly
called into question a number of important cultural values implicit to late
nineteenth century European society. These included the notion of the family as sacred and private; the patriarchal roots of society and family life; the
notion that children should obey and honor their parents; and, perhaps
most important, affectionate notions of the treatment of children. Freud's
assertions of sexual abuse in childhood may have been "truths" which were
too difficult to accept for the wider populace, therapists, and (eventually)
Freud himself. As Alice Miller (1984b) asks, in relation to the role that the
social context may have played in Freud's sudden turnaround in thinking,

> What might it have meant in practical terms if Freud had remained true to [his
> original] insight? If we picture his readers, the women of the bourgeoisie of
> that day, with their elegant long dresses that hid their ankles, and the men with
> their stiff white collars and faultlessly cut suits (for it hardly can be supposed
> that his books were read by the working class), it is not hard to imagine the
> outrage and indignation that would have greeted the facts presented above.
> The indignation would not have been directed against this form of child abuse
> per se but against the man who dared to speak about it. For most of these
> refined people were firmly convinced from an early age that only fine, noble,
> valiant, and edifying deeds (subjects) ought to be talked about publicly. (pp.
> 116–117)

In constructing a mythic theoretical design to account for children's
"fantasies" of sexual abuse, Alice Miller (1984b) and Jeffrey Masson (1984)
argue that Freud protected society from having to face up to the spectra of
sexual trauma in childhood. Within *this* interpretation of the history of the
psychoanalytic movement, the social and historical context of late nineteenth century European society directly impacted on and informed (with
potentially severe consequences to abused children) the conceptual assumptions which underlay early formulations of the psychoanalytic model of
childhood.

The Information-Processing Model of Childhood

The psychoanalytic example above presents a plausible but inconclusive
view of the mythic roots of developmental theory (since it is not known to
what degree the social context actually played a role in Freud's rejection of
the seduction theory). Perhaps the most explicit example of the role of myth
in developmental psychology arose in tandem with the computer age some

forty years ago. Beginning in the 1960s, some developmental theorists began to use the computer as a metaphor for human intelligence. In contrast
to Piaget's attempt to formulate an all-encompassing model of cognitive
development, information processing theorists sought to isolate the precise
sequence of logical steps which were required to complete specific cognitive
and problem-solving tasks. For these theorists, the application of computer
principles to human intelligence provided the best means for reducing complex intellectual tasks into their constituent parts (Siegler, 1983). The flow
of information through a computer system — from input device, to short-
term or working memory, to central processing unit, to long-term memory
and output device — was seen to be metaphorically equivalent to the sequence of operations in human cognition and problem-solving. This computer metaphor applied to all stages of child development, but the efficiency, complexity, and types of operations available to children developed
over time. Largely as a result of the linkage between this model of cognition
and computer technology, the information processing tradition has continued to evolve alongside even more recent technological advances in computer science (Gardner, 1991). Were it not for the invention of computers,
however, it is likely that the information processing tradition would never
have originally arisen. Hence the important role played by the social context in developmental psychology is made clear.

THE CULTURAL CONSTRUCTION OF CHILDHOOD:
A COSMOLOGICAL MODEL

Developmental psychology addresses only one of many aspects which make
up the sociohistorical construction of childhood. (Prior to the late nineteenth century, the discipline of child psychology as a formal institution did
not yet even exist.) Many factors other than theories of development also
inform the social and historical construction of childhood across time and
place. Until the mid–twentieth century, however, very few studies on the
cultural and historical construction of childhood existed. All this changed
in 1962 with the publication of Phillipe Aries's seminal work *Centuries of
Childhood: A Social History of Family Life*. Aries asserted that our modern
conception of childhood was not a static construction, but one that gradually developed and changed over time. Aries's argument was based largely
on his historical analysis of period paintings, which from the fall of the
Roman Empire until about the twelfth century depicted children engaged in
the same activities and wearing the same dress as adults, with no evidence
of a separate "culture of childhood." The passage below summarizes Aries's
conclusion that at one time in our history there was no conception of

childhood, but that "children" were nevertheless treated with warmth and fondness:

> In medieval society the idea of childhood did not exist; this is not to suggest that children were neglected, forsaken, or despised. The idea of childhood is not to be confused with affection for children: it corresponds to an awareness of the particular nature of childhood, that particular nature which distinguishes the child from the adult . . . as soon as the [medieval] child could live without the constant solicitude of his mother, his nanny or his cradle-rocker, he belonged to adult society. (p. 128)

Beginning in the fifteenth century, according to Aries, a new valuation of children arose. A concern for the moral integrity of childhood gradually began to develop, as did a renewed interest in the education of children. [Postman (1985) attributes the rise of schooling during this period to the invention of the printing press and the emergence of literacy as a new social force in the lives of children.] The modern ideal that the child required special treatment and was not yet ready for full and equal participation in the adult world began to take hold.

Although *Centuries of Childhood* remains a seminal work within the field of the social history of childhood, Aries's thesis that children were treated with affection throughout history (and were better off when there was no conception of childhood at all) has been disputed by a number of theorists who have chronicled the history of child abuse through the ages (e.g., Breiner, 1990). Chief among these theorists is Lloyd de Mause (1988), who begins his rebuke of Aries's argument with the following often quoted statement:

> The history of childhood is a nightmare from which we have only recently begun to awaken. The further back in history one goes, the lower the level of child care and the more likely children are to be killed, abandoned, beaten, terrorized, and sexually abused. (p. 1)

Working from a revised psychoanalytic perspective, de Mause traces the changing relationship between adults and children through time. He postulates that it is the adult's projection of his or her own unmet needs on the child which accounts for the extent of the brutality and exploitation of children that one encounters the further back one goes in history. In sharp contrast to Aries, de Mause argues that there has been a gradual improvement in the quality of relationships between adults and children as time has progressed. He identifies the modern recognition of childhood as a unique and vulnerable phase within the human life span as being critical to the humane treatment of children in contemporary society.

Like Aries, de Mause's ideas have also faced criticism. Melvin Konner (1991) challenges de Mause's conclusion that all past societies treated their children harshly. Konner points to anthropological studies of traditional cultures (which was beyond the scope of de Mause's analysis) to support his argument that (some) societies of the past did treat their children humanely. Paul Shepard (1982), whose conception of childhood will be reviewed in Chapter 4, agrees with de Mause that there are "profound psychic dislocations at the root of modern society" (p. xii) which may be traceable to child rearing practices of the past, but he also criticizes de Mause for failing to put forward an alternative healthy paradigm or archetype of childhood for comparison.

Controversies in the field of the social history of childhood and conflicting ideals over what exactly constitutes "childhood" beg the need for a comprehensive model of the cosmology of childhood which can account for differences in the sociohistorical construction of childhood across time and place. Figure 3.1 proposes such a model in a formative way. While no

Figure 3.1. The Cosmology of Childhood

The social and historical context

Peer culture

Growth and development   Inner life

The idea/role of the child and theories of development

Child-rearing approaches and socialization subpatterns

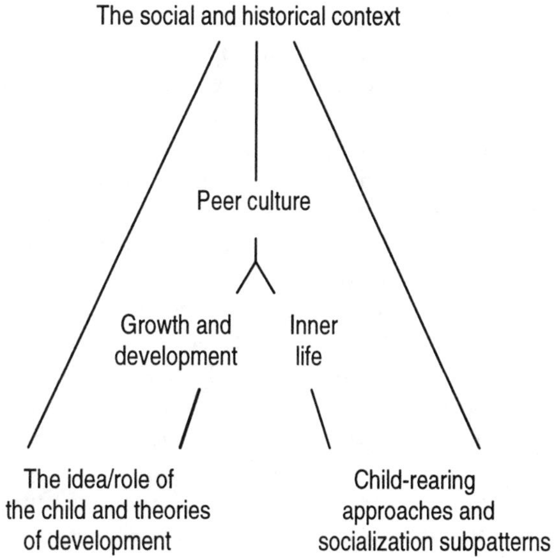

claims are made that this figure offers a complete view of the child, it is argued that the model does serve to highlight a number of important intrinsic and extrinsic factors which contribute to the cultural construction of childhood. Although each of these factors undoubtedly act on one another in a complex way, it is possible to address the unique aspects of each within the context of a "metaview" of the child.

The Social and Historical Context

What constitutes childhood and how children are treated and reared is largely informed by the social and historical context which places definite limits on institutional, social, and other forms of support for children. The arrangements (and very existence) of social institutions impact on the daily lives of children and inform the underlying role or place of the child in society. In cases where children live amid uncertainty and upheaval, sources of support may be tenuous at best, and possibly even nonexistent. In all cases, however, the social context is multifaceted and comprises a number of interwoven levels including family, community, nation, region, and world. Structural dimensions related to inequities in access to resources within and between these levels also inform the underlying social conditions of society.

The Idea/Role of the Child and Theories of Development

The idea of the child is integral to the cultural construction of childhood. Insofar as no distinction is made between "adults" and "children," no separate conception of childhood is possible. Children and adults are conceived of in the same way—they face the same challenges and responsibilities and are offered similar levels of support from social institutions. Within such a design, there may be no specific term or word to indicate "child" (for such a term would presuppose the existence of an idea of the child), no separate representation of the child in artistic endeavors, and no special status for young persons in the eyes of the law.

In a vast majority of cultures, an extended period of neoteny (childhood) is judged to be necessary for young people's mastery of the skills and knowledge base of society and their enculturation into the norms, values, and traditions of the culture. (This is just as true for many traditional societies as it is for highly technological societies.) In such societies there is an idea of the child, but exactly what this idea entails can vary dramatically across time and place. For example, the eighteenth century European romantic view of the child as inherently good and innocent arose in stark contrast to the sixteenth century puritanical vision of the child as born with original sin and prone to evil. However, in each case the "true nature" of the child was intricately related to other underlying religious and social visions of the time. From a complementary perspective, the economic and social value of children also varies across time and place, as Viviana A. Zelizer (1985) has shown, and impacts on the idea of children as economic and consumer resources.

That children be given a clear role in society seems to be a necessary precondition for ensuring children's inclusion and participation in the dominant patterns of social life, regardless of the social and historical context. Contemporary concerns in many industrialized countries that children (and particularly adolescents) lack a clear sense of direction and life purpose may be related to the lack of a clearly defined role for children and adolescents in society at present. In many cultures, rites of passage—specific acts or events which mark the transition from one life stage to another—serve to underscore the importance of achievements in childhood and adolescence and further indicate the role or place of the child in society.

Child Rearing Approaches and Socialization Subpatterns

Parenting styles and caregiving roles for adults differ across time and place, as do family size and composition. The institutional arrangements of families impact on child rearing practices, as in the example of communal-based approaches to child rearing in which adults from the wider community (in addition to the natural parents) hold primary care responsibilities for children. The history of child rearing practices in Western societies shows that the idea of the child, especially religious ideals of the child as born inherently "good" or "evil," have strongly influenced the affectionate versus callous treatment of children throughout the modern period (Greven, 1991). Beyond culture-wide notions of the child, however, are individual parental expectations for children, as well as other microlevel and familial factors which also influence child rearing approaches and point to wide discrepancies in child rearing practices within cultures. Contemporary research would seem to indicate that regardless of social context, a supportive, caregiving role for adults in the lives of children is necessary for subsequent healthy development and can be pivotal for children who are at risk of exposure to community violence and other dangers (Garbarino, 1992). (This is discussed in greater detail in Chapter 5.) Underlying the socialization process in stratified cultures are implicit socialization subpatterns which surreptitiously influence children's inculcation into society, lead to the differential treatment of persons within society, and serve to substantiate and perpetuate social inequities across generations (especially in terms of class, race, and gender).

Growth and Development

Despite the fact that they are largely a function of biology, genetics, and time-critical stage development, physical growth and psychological/social development can also be related to the cultural construction of childhood. Inadequate diet and nutrition can impact on physical growth and lead to low body weight and stunted growth for young children living in impoverished communities (UNICEF, 1993). In other respects, too, societal attitudes regarding body weight and physique can lead to variations in eating habits and exercise across cultures. Eating disorders such as anorexia nervosa and bulimia, for example, have arisen in large part due to the excessive value placed on thinness in Western societies (Brumberg, 1988). Also, there are striking cultural differences in patterns of physical development across time. During the last 150 years, the median age of menarche for American and European girls has dropped from a high of just over 17 years to just under 13 years of age (Tanner, 1978). As will be shown in Chapter 5, psychological development is also largely culturally constructed and is affected by variations in child rearing practices and social context, including exposure to community violence and other risk factors.

Peer Culture

When one moves beyond the restricted view that what constitutes childhood is solely imposed on children from without, it becomes clear that children are also active in the construction of childhood. As Wartofsky (1983) argues:

> The child is active in its own right, not simply imitatively, but as an *agent in its own construction*. And it is this probing, inventive, and curious child-activity that is the essential other aspect of the dialectical construction of childhood . . . Children are active . . . in the institutional-social forms that child-society provides: those invented and changing forms of peer organization and interaction, whether these be the games children play, or street-corner society, or the as-yet-mysterious and unexplored modes of cultural transmission of child-lore and child-humor . . . [Although] child activity and agency is itself essential in the actual construction of childhood . . . the child's possibilities of exercising and developing its modes of activity are subject to the constraints, influences, or opportunities that a particular social-historical context presents. (pp. 199–200, 203–204)

The ethnographic research conducted by Peter and Iona Opie (1959, 1969) in parks and playgrounds over several decades shows how important a role the peer group can play in shaping the "culture of childhood." In their exploration of the lore and language of school children, the Opies chronicled children's construction and mediation of social worlds apart from the worlds of adults, created for their own purposes, and intricately related to the oral culture of childhood. It is the incantations evoked by children, the games and rituals of childhood, and the negotiations between children on the playground which inform and underlie many of the meanings children give to the world. Often the structural foundations which underlie these incantations and games (e.g., hide-and-seek) are implicit in the play experiences of children from a wide variety of cultural backgrounds the world over. The apparent uniformity of child lore and the speed with which oral incantations can be transmitted over wide geographical areas also emerges as integral to the cosmology of childhood.

Inner Life

From both cognitive and affective/spiritual perspectives, the inner life of children and children's subjective experience of the world emerges as integral to the cosmology of childhood. How children make sense of the world, their intuitive thought processes, the meanings and causes which they attribute to phenomena, and their "folk theories" about how the world works in large part reflect the cognitive dimensions of children's interior life and help children to situate themselves within the context of surrounding physical and cultural conditions (e.g., see Coles, 1986). The philosophizing and witticisms of children also emerge within such a design (Matthews, 1980). From a complementary perspective, evocative peak experiences in childhood (Armstrong, 1985; Robinson, 1977) and the developmental processes of identification with adult caregivers, peer group, and place (Sobel, 1993) largely find expression within an affective/spiritual conception of the child's inner life. The emergence of a need for privacy and aloneness time as the child matures can serve to accentuate this process of identification and move the interior life of childhood to new levels of awareness.

TOWARD A FUNCTIONAL VISION OF CHILDHOOD

In this book it is argued that a constructivist thesis offers the most effective means for conceptualizing the cosmology of childhood. One of the advantages of such a position is that debates over the "true nature" of childhood are for the most part avoided and made unnecessary, since what constitutes childhood at any given time (or place) is seen to be culturally constructed by way of the factors outlined above. But such a relativistic thesis also leaves many questions unanswered. For example, no clear conception of what *should* constitute childhood is given, nor is any attempt made to suggest that certain constructions of childhood may be disadvantageous, regardless of the social and historical context. There are also ecological concerns here. Constructivism as a conceptual orientation is perhaps more prone than other, more organic epistemologies, to ignore or devalue the importance of our biological heritage upon which the cultural capacities of humans are built. Thus the biological and ecological feedback connections which connect humans to the wider earth community — our reliance on the chemical and life-giving processes of the planet, our need for clean air and water, our four billion years of biological heritage, the universal appeal of animals and nature throughout most of human history, and our ongoing efforts to articulate an ecosophical cosmology, etc. — together form a dialectical relationship between culture and nature that tends to remain unaddressed within most constructivist accounts, not unlike the importance of the ecological challenge itself.

The discussion below and the chapters which follow aim in part to rectify these omissions by arguing for a *functional* conception of childhood which (1) meets the physical and psychosocial needs of children (Chapter 5); (2) is congruent with the recovery of sustainable relations with the natural world (Chapters 4 and 6); and (3) further indicates the role or place of the child within this recovery (Chapter 6). It is argued that adults *do* have a moral obligation to build a better life for children and that this better life can be achieved in part by applying selected criteria (undoubtedly also culturally constructed) to contemporary conceptions of childhood.

Two assertions are made which establish the context for the remaining chapters. First, true to the argument of this book, it is maintained that the ecological crisis provides the overriding (although certainly not only) sociohistorical context at present, even despite other challenges facing the world. (The basis for this assertion was established in the first chapter. The ecological crisis is *global* in scope and growing increasingly *acute* in manifestation. Our hopes for a better future life for our children are now directly dependent on our ability to respond effectively to this crisis.)

Second, it is argued that children be given a clear role in the recovery of sustainable relations with the natural world. As noted earlier in this chapter, specifying the role or place of the child in society seems to be a necessary precondition for ensuring children's inclusion and participation in the dominant patterns of social life during any era. However, this may be particularly crucial at present. Perhaps at no other time in the history of Western civilization have children and adolescents been more excluded from participation in the dominant patterns of daily life than in contemporary society. (The efforts of advertisers and the mass media who cater to children as an increasingly lucrative consumer market represent important but unfortunately self-serving exceptions to this pattern of exclusion.) The development of a system of institutional mass schooling during the last century initially made this a potentiality, but it is the exclusion of children in contemporary society from the most integral aspects of daily life (save for the four walls of the classroom) that has made this a reality. As Gregory A. Smith (1992) argues, such a move is firmly grounded within some of the most alienating aspects of the modern, industrial worldview:

> In a variety of ways . . . schools have acted to consolidate and extend among their students a number of fundamental principles of the modern/industrial world view. By removing children from their homes, neighborhoods, and the surrounding nonhuman physical environment, schools have often led children to become increasingly detached from their own experience of the world . . . educators have then inducted students into social relations characterized primarily by the absence of sustained support or commitment. Children learn within the school that they are individuals, cut off from their teachers and most of their peers . . . The incentive for accepting these forms of detachment has been the promise of both economic mobility and social progress tied to the development of alternative forms of personal security, dependent not upon interpersonal commitments, but individual effort. (p. 70)

By going against a centuries-old apprenticeship-style approach to education rooted in the child's full (but not necessarily equal) participation in the dominant patterns of social life, the contemporary institutional arrangement of schools transcends even the most striking philosophical differences that can be made between the technocratic, progressive, and holistic positions discussed in Chapter 2. "Prior to the invention of the common school," continues Smith,

> most children learned about the natural and social worlds around them through their own investigations, through observing and imitating older children and adults, through play, through listening to stories, and through forms of instruction that were linked to the performance of necessary tasks. Although some learning occurred in the kinds of formal settings we associate with modern schools—especially learning related to the mastery of religious lore or texts—most children learned by actively participating in the life of their society. (p. 54)

In moving away from a participative approach to education, the traditional mentorship role played by adults in the lives of children—a potentially rich and varied role in which adult support was not only explicit, but also tacit—has largely given way to a crude, systematized caricature of its former self in the form of the classroom teacher (who in turn faces her own constraints in dealing with increasing numbers of students). It is perhaps ironic that this potentially evolutionary "wrong turn" in the development of a formalized system of education now provides us with the needed institutional structure upon which to base a cultural reorientation of society via a new ecological mandate for schools. (The decentralized vision of education inherent to an apprenticeship-style approach to learning may not have provided us with this same opportunity, yet such a vision could still represent a viable future goal once the most integral aspects of the cultural reorientation have occurred.[2])

Implicit to such a formalized view of education is the necessity of discovering alternative avenues within which children can play an integral role in society. A variation of Margaret Mead's notion of *prefigurative cultures* (1978) may provide us with an important clue as to how this might effectively occur. Mead used this term in reference to her prediction of a new sociological arrangement in rapidly changing societies in which traditional adult/child socialization patterns would be reversed and children would begin to play a key role in adult resocialization. Working from the vantage point of the Technozoic perspective, Mead argued that as modern society became even more highly technologized, children's plasticity of response to change would allow them to adapt more easily to new technologies, and, as a result, place them in a teaching relationship to adults. (What Mead didn't take into account, however, was the potentially alienating aspects of this new technology which has in some respects served to further erode adult/child associations, and, perhaps more generally, community life.) If considered from a somewhat different perspective, Mead's assertions can also be related to an Ecozoic view of change. The child's plasticity of response to change, her "natural" aptitude for wonder, and her need to frame an initial relationship to the world could together serve as the catalyst for a more comprehensive reorientation to the natural world within the general population. Certainly such capacities could provide a pivotal point of intervention for building a new relationship to the wider earth community within the next generation. However, for such a plan to be successful it would first be necessary to counter the problematic notion of progressive and incremental change in childhood (critiqued earlier in this chapter) which subtly denigrates the unique capacities of children. Only then could children's role in the recovery of sustainable relations with the wider earth community likely be appreciated fully.

One hopeful sign is that increasingly, people are coming to discover that there is an inherent quality of experience that is unique to childhood and perhaps even critical to the human role in the recovery of sustainable relations with the natural world. The child as messenger is a common theme within the epistemology of this growing body of educators, poets, holistic theorists, traditional storytellers, spiritualists, and elders. Their stories, handed down over centuries, are presently being critically related to the challenges facing the earth and the human at the close of the twentieth century. As with the developmental theories noted in this chapter, these stories, too, are cultural constructions of reality, but their abiding virtue may be that they delineate a functional role for the child in the recovery of sustainable relations with the natural world. We next turn to an in-depth exploration of several such holistic conceptions of childhood.

CHAPTER 4

The Story of Childhood:
A New Interpretation and Retelling

Childhood as a lifephase is becoming at home in the world.
—Donald Vandenberg, *Being and Education* (1971)

We have explored the ideological underpinnings of the environmental impasse in terms of crises in ecology, economics, and consciousness. In Chapter 2, this discussion was applied to three contemporary philosophies of education which inform much public discourse on educational practice. Although each philosophy was found wanting, it was argued that only the holistic philosophy forwarded a viable program for reform in light of the environmental challenges we presently face. Now the discussion moves beyond the critique mode and further develops this thesis by focusing on a variety of holistic perspectives on development in middle childhood, in preparation for an exploration of specific educational practices and holistic curricula in Chapter 5.

One of the primary purposes of this chapter is to demonstrate that far from needing to be rescued from obscurity, a holistic and ecologically sensitive view of child development in fact has a long, rich history extending back at least to the eighteenth century. Despite having been largely ignored (and devalued) by the more mainstream movements in child psychology (e.g., the psychoanalytic, cognitive-developmental, and information processing traditions), developmental theorists working within the traditions of holism have amassed an impressive array of perspectives on child development, and in numerous cases have been able to test and further develop such perspectives in practice.

Holistic developmental theory differs from mainstream positions in child psychology in a number of important ways. First, by incorporating a spiritual element into their work, many holistic theorists purport to address a broader conception of "the child" than does traditional developmental psychology. Holistic theorists can lay claim to having explored significant aspects of childhood experience heretofore untouched by the more mainstream positions. For example, research into peak experiences in childhood [see Robinson (1977) and Armstrong (1984)] reveals certain potentialities in children that could have significant ramifications for our conceptions of childhood in the future.

Of course, a broader view of the child presents its own difficulties as well. Holistic theory rarely paints as detailed a picture of childhood as does mainstream developmental psychology. Moreover, holistic theorists seldom subscribe to a mechanistic or reductionist view of growth in childhood. Therefore their theories are not so easily tested in the rigorously controlled conditions demanded by experimental science. (In contrast to many mainstream studies, holistic research is often conducted in the natural environments and contexts in which the behavior under study occurs.) Significantly, many holistic theorists do not aim to defeat the mainstream positions in child psychology; rather, by focusing on phenomena and aspects of experience unaccounted for within mainstream developmental theory, they see their work as providing either a complementary focus to the efforts of mainstream theorists or an integrative context in which mainstream developmental psychology is but one aspect of a larger picture. Thomas Armstrong (1985), for example, has argued that there are in fact two lines of development in childhood — one occurring "from the body up" and another "from the spirit down" which account for both the mainstream and holistic positions respectively.

A second distinction between holistic and mainstream theory concerns differences in the methodological and research tools used by mainstream and holistic theorists. In contrast to the carefully controlled experimental conditions championed by many mainstream researchers, holistic theorists use a wide variety of qualitative investigative tools including ethnographic (participant observation) research, narratives and journal writing, case studies, interpretive analyses of children's drawings and paintings, and the autobiographical reflections of adults. Generally speaking, holistic theorists shy away from a restricted focus on research which yields supposedly "objective" and quantifiable results; rather a premium is placed on the importance of subjective experience (for both participant and researcher) and the interpretative role of the theorist in forming conclusions based on the findings.

One further distinction between mainstream and holistic developmental theory seems particularly noteworthy, given the subject matter of this book. Whereas mainstream theory has traditionally focused on human–human relationships and the child's manipulation of the outside world, certain traditions within holistic theory have begun to address the potentially important socializing role that the natural world may play in human development. Far from disassociating the child from the nurturing aspects of the natural world, holistic developmental theorists such as Edith Cobb (1977) and Paul Shepard (1982) have articulated a new biocentric vision of development in childhood. This is in stark contrast to the implicit anthropocentricism which even today plagues most mainstream (and some holistic) theories of development.

This last point is most significant for the discussion at present. At precisely the moment in history when the validity of our political, economic, scientific, legal, medical, educational, and other institutions are being called into question because of their role in contributing to the environmental impasse, it seems particularly fitting that we should also carefully consider the ideological and other cultural assumptions which underlie and inform such institutions. Perhaps one of the most conspicuous of these assumptions is the notion that the wider earth community need play no role in supporting human growth and development across the life span. On the face of it, this may in fact appear to be true. As a species, we have survived for several centuries now, seemingly disassociated from the most integral aspects of the natural world. Yet, as indicated in Chapter 1, this has in itself contributed to our current predicament and presently threatens our ability to secure a viable future world for our children. The task before us seems to be one of reacquainting ourselves with those "teachings" of the earth community that can help us to bring our human institutions and endeavors in line with the inherent needs of a threatened natural world. Beginning to apprehend how this can most effectively occur in childhood, during that most receptive period in the human life cycle, is the focus of this chapter.

MIDDLE CHILDHOOD AND THE SEARCH FOR A FUNCTIONAL COSMOLOGY OF THE UNIVERSE

Despite major variations in focus and interpretation, most mainstream and holistic developmental theorists identify a common set of key transition stages in childhood and adolescence (see Table 4.1). Within both traditions, the period of prenatal development has historically received only scant attention. Recently, however, the critical importance of this stage for subsequent healthy development has become more widely understood, as has the importance of the perinatal stage of birth itself. Sharp rises in the number of cases of "crack babies" and newborns inflicted with fetal alcohol syndrome tragically underscore the importance of the fetal growth stage. Likewise the importance of an adequate maternal diet during pregnancy

Table 4.1. Developmental Milestones in Mainstream and Holistic Theories of Development

Developmental Stage	Ages	Ushered in by
Prenatal development	Conception–Birth	Conception
Infancy & early childhood	Birth–6	Birth
Middle childhood	6–12	Loss of the milk teeth
Adolescence	12–18	Onset of puberty

and the emotional state of the mother is becoming more widely studied and understood.

The periods of infancy and early childhood comprise (in part) the stage-critical tasks of learning to walk and talk which provide the biological foundations for later development. The acquisition of language is critical, not only for communicative competence and social interaction, but also for the development of higher (symbolic) reasoning skills and the further refinement of "self." Likewise, learning to walk not only provides for increased mobility, but also spurs exploratory behavior and further enhances gross and fine motor coordination and the skills of object manipulation.

According to a variety of developmental theories, the transition to middle childhood occurs at the age of six or seven. Age seven, for example, marks the transition to concrete operations in Piaget's cognitive developmental theory (Piaget, 1973) and signals a "brain spurt" in Joseph Chilton Pearce's theory of development. Pearce (1992) writes that:

> around age six or seven . . . nature provides another massive brain growth spurt to accommodate the new intelligences unfolding . . . The six-year-old's brain is two-thirds of its adult size with five to seven times more neural connections and available fields than it had in early childhood or will have as an adult. Nature provides an abundance of material for the vast potentials available in the new operations. (p. 174)

For some holistic theorists, including Rudolf Steiner and Maria Montessori, it is the loss of the milk teeth around age seven which marks the transition to a new stage of development and consciousness. For Steiner

(1924/1974), this singular event signals the completion of the "moulding" processes of early childhood. A number of other physical changes also occur at this age: the loss of the baby fat and rounded contours of early childhood; the increase in height and thinness; and the strengthening of the bone structure (Standing, 1957/1984). Beyond these physiological changes, however, lies the equally substantive psychological changes which usher in a new relationship to the world. Middle childhood functions as a period of consolidation, but it also introduces new capacities and potentialities not evident in earlier childhood.

Striving For Independence and Self-Identity. The child's entry into middle childhood is marked by an increase in the differentiation of self from others. New challenges, such as the first day of school, confront the child and signal her entry into a wider social world. The child seeks approval from others (especially peers) on the basis of her strengths and uniqueness. There is a greater capacity for the self-management of behavior as impulsivity decreases and knowledge of the self, emotions, and self-regulatory processes increases (Collins, 1984). A need for privacy emerges as an important consideration in the middle to late periods of this stage.

Exercising New Powers of Cognition. The child demonstrates higher reasoning skills in thinking about increasingly multifaceted problems and situations which confront her in both the physical and social worlds. She demonstrates an increased capacity for dealing with conceptual representations of objects and events (Collins, 1984) and is able to take on the perspectives of others. Metacognitive thought processes ("thinking about thinking") gradually develop, as do planning and organizational skills. Reflective observation serves as an important tool for analyzing situations and solving problems.

Building Friendships With Peers; Learning to Satisfy Psychological Needs Within the Context of Group Life. The peer group emerges as a basic social unit. There is a decided shift away from family and to peers as the basis for satisfying belonging and actualization needs. (However, the support and security afforded by the primary caregivers and the home environment are still essential.) Playground games provide opportunities for children to learn about social systems and relationships, develop a knowledge of social conventions, and experiment with and rehearse strategies for maintaining and extending friendships with peers (Collins, 1984). In the early stages of middle childhood, play is fluid, open ended, and unstructured. Gradually, as games become more organized, negotiation, compromise, fair play, and rule-defining become increasingly important. Children "spend half [their] time in passionate argument about fairness," writes Pearce (1992), "the other half in play—but it is *all* equally play" (p. 163).

Searching For Meaningfulness and Purpose in the World of Nature and in the Physical and Cultural Worlds That Surround the Child. Among other achievements, children are genetically mandated in early childhood to learn how to walk and talk. Walking, coupled with the enhancement of gross and fine motor skills, provides the foundations not only for mobility, but also for the *physical* manipulation of the external world. Similarly, the acquisition of language skills in early childhood provides the foundations for the *symbolic* (i.e., semantic) manipulation of the inner (subjective) and outer (intersubjective) world of meanings. During middle childhood, children apply these newfound powers to the tasks of apprehending and transforming the wider physical and symbolic worlds that surround them. Concurrently and on an increasingly conscious level, children begin to attend to the norms, values, cultural stories, and traditions of the wider culture. Middle childhood, writes James Fowler (1981), is the stage in which the child

> begins to take on for him- or herself the stories, beliefs, and observances that symbolize belonging to his or her community . . . In this stage the rise of concrete operations leads to the curbing and ordering of the previous stage's imaginative composing of the world. The episodic quality of [early childhood] gives way to a more linear, narrative construction of coherence and meaning. Story becomes the major way of giving unity and value to experience. This is the faith of the school child . . . [who] composes a world based on reciprocal fairness and an immanent justice based on reciprocity. The actors in their cosmic stories are anthropomorphic. They can be affected deeply and powerfully by symbolic and dramatic materials and can describe in endlessly detailed narrative what has occurred . . . The new capacity or strength in this stage is the rise of narrative and the emergence of story, drama, and myth as ways of finding and giving coherence to experience. (p. 149)

It is the argument of this book that in the same way that there is a critical period for the emergence of language in early childhood, there is also a time-critical stage of development between the ages of about 6 and 12 whereby the child comes to co-construct a functional cosmology of the universe—a "working theory" of the world. The foundations for such a cosmology are initially laid down during early childhood, but it is through the new capacities of middle childhood that such a cosmology is first articulated in a formative way. The child's maturing sense of self and newfound powers of cognition, coupled with her strivings for a functional cosmology of the universe, mark her entry into a new relationship with the world—a relationship built on a reciprocity between the child and the world of nature and the physical and cultural worlds that surround her.

The child's search for a functional cosmology of the universe is inherently a search for meaningfulness and purpose in the world. As outlined in Chapter 2, this search is congruent with the holistic vision for education. Yet just as important, it is chronicled by a number of holistic developmental theorists, many of whom consider middle childhood to be pivotal, not only to the subsequent healthy development of the individual, but also to the recovery of sustainable relations with the natural world. The discussion below emerges from this child/nature/culture perspective and situates middle childhood within the context of selected aspects of several holistic theories of development. This sets the stage for an overview of a methodology and curriculum for an ecologically sensitive approach to education in middle childhood in Chapter 6.

CHILDREN, NATURE, AND CONSCIOUSNESS: SELECTED CONSTRUCTIONS OF MIDDLE CHILDHOOD

The roots of both the progressive and holistic conceptions of childhood can be traced back to the eighteenth century Age of Romanticism and the educational visions advanced by Jean-Jacques Rousseau (1712–1778) and Swiss educator Johann Heinrich Pestalozzi (1746–1827). Both argued that within the newborn child were the seeds of later intelligence and personality. The aim of education was to follow carefully the natural stages of growth in childhood and allow for the full development of each child's potential by stimulating and nurturing his[1] inherent capacities. For Rousseau (1762/1979), direct sensory contact with the natural world in both early and middle childhood was critical to the healthy development of personality. Pestalozzi was similarly influenced by this sentiment and incorporated important elements of Rousseau's philosophy into his educational experiments at Burgdorf (1800–1804) and Yverdun (1805–1825). Through his lessons in map and model-making, for example, Pestalozzi pioneered the study of "place" in childhood by having his students explore the terrain and topography of local ecosystems (Curtis and Boultwood, 1956). However, it was left up to one of Pestalozzi's most respected student teachers to consolidate the child/nature relationship in an even more integral manner.

Friedrich Froebel (1782–1852)

As Pestalozzi's most influential protégé, German-born educator Friedrich Froebel further developed the relationship between the child and nature as established by Pestalozzi and Rousseau and introduced into this mix an

even more profound third dimension which embraced a threefold relatedness between humanity, nature, and spirit (God). Froebel is perhaps best
known as the founder of the kindergarten. Progressive education appropriated this aspect of his pedagogy (Karier, 1986), but dismissed those
elements of his work which extended from the spiritual realm and potentially threatened a secular view of education. Holistic education, on the
other hand, embraced Froebel's conception of the spirit and further developed it as the basis for a new vision of child development and education.

Froebel's theory of child development was deeply rooted in evolutionary discourse — a discourse directed by his conception of the spiritual realm
as a universal creative force that manifests itself within all of nature, including humankind. Within this context, Froebel's understanding of God was
not Christian in the ordinary sense, but ecological, for he perceived all of
nature as comprising the inherent make-up of God. Indeed, God was the
binding factor or unifying force between humankind and the balance of
nature, the animate and inanimate, empowering both nature and mind. In
a passage reminiscent of the Michelet quotation from Chapter 3, Froebel
(1826/1912) wrote that

> to the vulgar, superficial view, nature consists of many different and separate
> things, each with its own peculiar and independent character and purpose, and
> giving no indication of an inner bond of connection . . . But this cannot satisfy
> the human mind even in childhood, for that mind is itself one and undivided.
> So the child instinctively searches for unity in the diverse objects he perceives.
> He is gratified when he begins to find it, but only when he has fully grasped it
> is his spirit really content. (p. 102)

For Froebel, the inner world of the child was a reflection of the outer
world of nature. Self and object were at one and the same time separate
entities, yet also constituent parts of a total reality. Lilley (1967) writes that
Froebel

> saw a reciprocity between the self and the objects of its perception; as they are
> distinct entities this relationship is one of *separateness*, but as they have the
> same primary cause and the same essential character it is also one of *identity*
> . . . Therefore, each individual is both autonomous and self-active and also
> bound in association with everything else in the great chain of being. (pp. 9,
> 20; emphasis added)

"In Froebel's view," Lilley continues, "the human being is always in
relationship and every association is formative" (p. 23). Development proceeds in terms of finite adjustments to the individual's relationship to the
external conditions of the world. In this way, Froebel wrote, "the first
recognition that the self is distinct from its surroundings is quickly followed

by a longing to understand the life and language of the external world, and particularly of nature, and to take it up into the self's own life" (1826/1912, p. 132). This is perhaps Froebel's most significant contribution to the argument of this chapter. In middle childhood there emerges the capacity to recognize (and celebrate) the autonomy of the individual while subtly preserving the unity of selfhood and world. It remains within the task of middle childhood to build upon the child's primary powers of perception and further refine his sense of self—"in a word, to extend his mental horizon," wrote Froebel (p. 69)—but this is done not in isolation from the external world, but in relationship to its nurturing capacities and the diversity of experiences it affords.

In middle childhood, where local conditions permit, such a diversity of experience is largely mediated through direct sensory contact with the natural world. Froebel wrote that the child

> should early view and recognize the objects of nature in their true relations and original connections; he should learn by his longer walks to know his own neighborhood from beginning to end; he should roam through the adjoining country; he should accompany his brook or little river along its course from its source to its mouth, and observe the local differences in respect to the soil; he should wander about on the heights that the ramifications of the mountains may be plain to him; he should climb to the highest points, that he may survey the connection of the whole surrounding country, and be able to describe it to himself . . . By his own observation and his own discovering, by his own notice of this continuous and vivid coherence of nature, by the direct view of nature itself, not by explanations in words and ideas for which the boy has no intuition, there shall dawn upon him early, and, however dimly at the beginning, yet more and more clearly, the great thought of the inner, continual, vivid connection of all things and phenomena in nature. (pp. 234–235)

Froebel cautions us, however, that without proper adult guidance, the most important offerings of the natural world will remain hidden to the child. "It is true that children run about in fields and forests," Froebel wrote (p. 101), but they do not in themselves, "truly live in and with nature." Rather, it is the adult's role to mediate the child's experience of the natural world in a way that brings forth those essential elements of experience of nature we should wish to cultivate in the young. Careful observation of the natural world, the descriptive and nonformal naming of objects in nature, grouping natural items according to various classification schemes developed by the child, and the uncovering of relationships between objects in nature—all of these strategies are noted by Froebel for nurturing in the child a strong sense of continuity with the natural world.

The careful study of nature readily affords for a spatial view of reality, but it does not in itself satisfy the temporal longings of the child who searches for the causes of things and strives to establish a personal history for himself. Froebel argued that a focus on the present,

> with all the richness in occupation which it offers, is not enough. The fact of the present brings home to the child that there must have been a past. So the child wants to know what it was, that he may find in it the causes of what now exists. He wants the remains of the past to tell him their story, that he may know why they exist and in what circumstances they came into being. The child seeks this information from those around him, and so there develops in him the desire for story and legend, and, later on, for history. (p. 72)

What significance does Froebel attribute to story in middle childhood? In early childhood, it was enough for the young child to hear the same story over and over again, despite knowing it by heart. In middle childhood, story becomes a primary vehicle for building a functional cosmology of the universe. The narrative mode establishes a sense of continuity to existence and addresses the temporal basis of the child's search for meaningfulness and purpose in the world. "Innumerable questions burst from the child's inquiring soul, athirst for knowledge," wrote Froebel, "How? Why? When? What for? . . . The motive-force is the desire to seek and find the new, and bring to light the hidden" (pp. 68–69).

In exploring the pivotal role of fable, legend, myth, and fairy tale in forming character and engaging the child's imagination, Froebel wrote that for the child,

> the necessary points of comparison are given by the lives of others. In them the child can see, as it were, an image of his own active life, and so can measure its worth . . . its origin, its nature, and its outcome . . . Here we find the chief reason why the child has such a love for stories, legends, and fairy-tales, especially when they have a semblance of truth, or are at least within the limits of probability which he recognizes . . . The story may present strange men and strange lands, other times and other manners; yet in it the hearer seeks and finds an image of himself, even if no one else could say "That is like you" . . . Stirred by the reality of the events, the child listens intently, and finds in each such story a new treasure and a new conquest, adding to his own life whatever it offers him of instruction and inspiration. (pp. 148–149, 151)

Froebel was among the first interpreters of the child to recognize the pivotal role of the narrative mode in middle childhood, but in the 200 years since Froebel first laid down his thoughts, many holistic developmental theorists have followed his lead and further clarified the important role story plays in building a sense of meaningfulness and purpose in middle childhood. Among these theorists is Maria Montessori, who, despite being strongly influenced by Froebel, challenged his interpretation of the narrative mode in middle childhood. We next turn to Montessori's conception of middle childhood and her criticisms of Froebel.

Maria Montessori (1870–1952)

"The mind awakens in the face of creation," Montessori wrote of middle childhood (1948/1973, p. 64). The founder of the most widespread independent school movement in North America, Montessori originally trained in Italy as a medical doctor (she was the first woman MD to graduate from the University of Rome) before gaining a sound reputation and international following for her work with developmentally challenged and non-handicapped preschool children. Unique among holistic developmental theorists, Montessori developed a theory of child development and method of instruction that extend in large part from a clinical and empirically disciplined study of the child rooted in her scientific background in psychiatry and anthropology. Although best known for her work with younger children, Montessori also articulated a holistic vision of development and education in middle childhood which in recent years has found expression in a variety of elementary schools, including a growing number of public schools, throughout North America.

For Montessori, middle childhood functions as a period of consolidation, but also introduces new capacities and potentialities which were not evident in earlier childhood. Montessori argued that middle childhood comprises the "sensitive period" for the imagination. In early childhood, the child built up her mind and senses, first at the level of the unconscious (which Montessori termed the "absorbent mind"), and later through the willful manipulation of concrete materials in a prepared environment. With the transition to middle childhood, however, there arises within the child a need to exercise new modes of thought rooted within the child's newfound creative powers of imagination. In this way, argued Montessori, the passage from the first to the second stage of childhood is manifested by the move from the "motion in body" of early childhood to the "motion in thought" of middle childhood:

> Let us draw a parallel here with the smaller children who by touching objects trained their hand to greater dexterity. The exercise seemed to satisfy something inside of them. Touching for the younger child is what imagining is for the older one. On the former age level we would have worked on the sensorial plane as, for the latter, we work on the level of the imagination. (1948/1973, pp. 38–39)

The awakening of the imagination in middle childhood also signals an important shift in consciousness and the birth of the abstract powers of the intellect. The child has moved from a primarily biological and physically grounded period of development in infancy and early childhood into a new creative and symbolic mode of relatedness to the world rooted in the child's absorption of culture. Montessori argued that

> education between the ages of six and twelve is not a direct continuation of that which has gone before, though [it is] to be built on that basis. Psychologically there is a decided change in personality, and we recognize that nature has made this a period for the acquisition of culture, just as the former was for the absorption of environment. We are confronted with a considerable development of consciousness that has already taken place, but now that consciousness is thrown outward with a special direction, intelligence being extroverted, and there is an unusual demand on the part of the child to know the reasons of things. (1948/1967, p. 4)

For Montessori, the child's need to "know the reasons of things" is ultimately related to the child's broader search for a functional cosmology of the universe. Implicit to such a search is an expressed need on the part of the child to understand the world for himself and to exercise his own powers of judgment:

> An inner change has taken place, but nature is quite logical in arousing now in the child not only a hunger for knowledge and understanding, but a claim to mental independence. (1948/1967, p. 6)

Montessori argued that the child's inquiry into the inner workings of the universe is rooted within his natural inquisitiveness, in his growing sense of awareness of the nature of cause and effect, and perhaps most significantly, in his appeal to the grandeur and mystery of the universe as a whole. At the risk of foreshadowing later discussion in this chapter, it is perhaps not too much to say that Montessori viewed the child as longing "to possess the whole world as his theater of perception" (Cobb, 1977, p. 55). In middle childhood, observed Montessori (1948/1973, p. 12), "one of the most curious characteristics to be observed is the interest that occurs in the child when he begins to perceive things which he previously failed to notice." The child's expanding horizons take him well beyond the physical limits of a prepared environment, but also propel him into a wider (cultural) field of thought than that afforded to the younger child. In this way, argued Montessori (1948/1967, p. 4), middle childhood serves as the period for the "acquisition of culture, whereas the former was for the absorption of environment."

Montessori argued that the child's newfound engagement to the world calls for a special quality of relationship on the part of the teacher and a new kind of subject matter that appeals to the child's imagination. In many respects, Montessori's vision for education served to broaden and systematize Froebel's vision of childhood and theory of instruction reviewed earlier. For example, both educators saw the natural world as providing infinite possibilities for engaging the child's imagination. Yet despite this and a number of other similarities between their two systems of education,[2] Montessori was critical of Froebel's conception of the narrative mode in middle childhood. Like Froebel, Montessori recognized the pivotal role that the narrative mode plays in establishing a sense of continuity to existence and addressing the temporal basis of the child's search for meaningfulness and purpose in the world; but whereas Froebel attributed an important role to fairy tales and fantasy stories in this regard, Montessori argued that the cultivation of imagination in middle childhood should be intricately bound up with the enhancement of the child's understanding of the external conditions of the *real* world. She challenged Froebel's "escapist" notions of the fantasy world of childhood as being largely removed and alienated from reality, and juxtaposed against the developmental needs of children, and instead advocated the telling of the "universe story" as a way of situating children within the context of real world phenomena. Montessori (1948/1967) argued that an imagination which is

> cultivated by fairy tales [is] concerned with a world that is certainly full of marvels, but not the world around [us] in which [we] live. Certainly these tales have impressive factors which move the childish mind to pity and horror, for they are full of woe and tragedy, of children who are starved, ill-treated, abandoned, and betrayed. Just as adults find pleasure in tragic drama and literature, these tales of goblins and monsters give pleasure and stir the child's imagination, but they have no connection with reality. On the other hand, by offering the child the story of the universe, we give him something a thousand times more infinite and mysterious to reconstruct in his imagination, a drama no fable can reveal. (p. 16)

"Not only can imagination travel through infinite space," argued Montessori (1948/1967, p. 14), "but also through infinite time; we can go backward through the epochs and have the vision of the earth as it was, with the creatures that inhabited it." In Montessori schools, such a vision provides the context for much of the subject matter of the elementary curriculum and serves as the launching point for the child's inquiry into the wonders of the universe—both past and present:

> [Now] the Cosmic Plan can be presented to the child, as a thrilling tale of the earth we live in, its many changes through slow ages when water was Nature's

chief toiler for accomplishment of her purposes, how land and sea fought for supremacy, and how equilibrium of elements was achieved, that Life might appear on the stage and play its part in the great drama. (p. 2)

"When you say 'in the beginning' to a young child," writes David Kahn (1980, p. 12), "eyebrows raise. The 6-year-old immersed in the story of his own growth finds certain native interest in the origins and growth of his world." Montessori believed that the telling of the universe story not only engaged the child's imagination, but also satisfied a need within the child to discover her own personal growth and development to be an extension of the origins of the universe itself. As Kahn (1991) argues, Montessori recognized that:

the narrative model is built on a philosophical premise that questions deal not only with facts, but with origins, with issues of life and death, and, most importantly, that questions relate to the emotional needs of children to understand and explore their biological and psychological connection to the natural world and their cultures. (p. 6)

At about the time the Montessori movement was beginning to build up strength during the early decades of the twentieth century, another European educational reform movement was just beginning to take shape, inspired largely by the teachings of Austrian scientist and spiritualist Rudolf Steiner. Although in many respects juxtaposed in emphasis and design, both movements expressed a cardinal principle of holistic education which, as Montessori's granddaughter explained nearly seventy years later, was a fundamental respect for the multifaceted subtleties of the growing child. We turn to Rudolf Steiner's vision of middle childhood in the discussion below.

Rudolf Steiner (1861–1925)

Although there is no evidence to suggest that they ever met, Rudolf Steiner was a contemporary of Maria Montessori's. An eclectic writer and lecturer, Steiner was in touch with people from many walks of life. His contributions to the fields of art and architecture, agriculture, and theology are all well documented. However, it is Steiner's endeavors related to education which have perhaps had the most pervasive influence. In 1919, he founded the first Waldorf school (so named for the factory in which it was situated) in Stuttgart, Germany. Today the Waldorf movement numbers over 400 schools in some 20 countries and represents to many the richest living example of holistic education in practice.

Whereas Montessori's theory of development and education was largely rooted in her clinical and empirically disciplined study of the child within the environment of the classroom, Rudolf Steiner argued that his understanding of the child (and other phenomena) emerged from a super-sensory awareness of a spiritual world well beyond the material physical world which informed much of the scientific thinking of his time. It was Steiner's lifelong aim to bring the spiritual/artistic and materialistic/scientific communities closer together. Indeed, it is this spirit which perhaps best characterizes the fundamental philosophy of the Waldorf school movement right up to the present time.

Fundamental to Steiner's understanding of the growing child was his rejection of the mind/matter dualism to which most mainstream developmental theorists of his day subscribed. Conventional wisdom held that physical and psychological growth were generally best dealt with as separate matters, rather than as integrated and mutually complementary processes of development. In rejecting this principle, and also the often unscrutinized assumption that consciousness was centered solely in the human head, Steiner strove to better understand the role played by various physiological systems, beyond the brain and nervous system, in the psychological and spiritual development of the child. He paid particular attention to the importance of the limb and respiratory systems.

Steiner's notion of the "threefold person," comprising the processes of *thinking, feeling*, and *willing*, was central to his understanding of the integrative processes of physical and spiritual/psychological growth. Steiner compared thinking to a waking state in which the mind is alert and fully conscious. From the viewpoint of physical development, thinking is channeled through the brain and nervous system. Feeling is analogous to a dreaming state in which consciousness is only partially revealed, in a pictorial, rhythmic, or dreamlike form. Steiner argued that because of their cyclical and rhythmic nature, the respiratory and circulatory systems embody the faculty of feeling. Finally, the faculty of will is rooted in the limb system and is analogous to a sleeping state in which actions occur almost instinctively.

Following from the above analogies, Steiner argued that growth in childhood occurs both from the "body down" and the "spirit up." As children are born "awake" in the limbs and senses, it is the faculty of will which first finds expression in the psychological development of the young child. Young children learn best through direct and immediate contact with the outer world, and through the faculty of imitation. So too the regulation of gross and fine motor skills emerges as a major goal during the first years of life. As the child matures, psychological development moves up through the body, gradually reaching the head with the unfolding of the analytical powers of early adolescence. Steiner argued that from a complementary perspective, the physical development of the young child begins first with the head (which nearly reaches its full adult size by age 7) and works its way down as the child matures, gradually reaching the limb system with the growth spurt of adolescence.

Steiner believed that it was during middle childhood that the inner and outer forces of physical and conscious growth crossed paths to reveal the "heart of childhood"—a venerable period of artistic expression, rich inner life, and imagination. In middle childhood, writes John Davy (1973), Steiner regarded

> the rhythmic functions of the body, which are embodied most explicitly in the heart and lungs, as the organic basis of our emotional life, as the limbs are the basis for action and the brain for thought. Thus while the pre-school child lives essentially in the immediate events around him, the seven-year-old begins to dispose of a freer life of imagination and feeling, with which he can enter into painting, story-telling, or games in a new way. At this time, thought is not naturally critical and analytic, but pictorial and dramatic.

Contrast this with the consciousness of the younger child (Harwood, 1958),

> which extends beyond the sphere of his little body. [He] actually lives *into* his immediate surroundings in a way incomprehensible to the adult; his life of thought and feeling is not personal, but is intimately bound up with the life, speech and actions of those who surround him . . . In an impersonal dream-like, or rather sleep-like way, his powers of consciousness are living in his environment. (pp. 15–16)

Steiner argued that as the young child matures, this immersive experience of the world gradually gives way to a more reciprocal relationship to the world in middle childhood in which the autonomy of self is increasingly maintained. But this is a gradual process which unfolds slowly over time. In sharp contrast to conventional thinking, Steiner (1924a/1982) believed that up to even the ninth year, the child is still

> not in a position to distinguish clearly between himself and the outside world; even in his feeling life, the feeling of the world and the feeling of his own ego are not clearly distinguished . . . he looks upon what goes on outside him as a continuation of his own being. (p. 81)

During this early stage of middle childhood, the child's affinity for the world translates into an almost instinctive faith in and reverence towards the adults in the child's life, a kind of heightened need for surrogacy. Essentially, Steiner argued, the child is calling for an authoritative response on

the part of the adult caregiver who can best imbue a sense of confidence
and goodness with which the child can identify and absorb. Here Steiner's
notion of authority was not pedantic and dictatorial, but compassionate
and benevolent. His assertions on authority did not extend from any specific sociological observations or ideological viewpoint, but rather from
what he perceived to be an expressed need on the part of the child to find in
the adult caregiver, the sources of support and guardianship needed for
healthy development. (We revisit this point in Chapter 5.)

As the child approaches the age of about nine or ten, an inner change
takes place in his developing ego-consciousness, so that "at this moment of
life the child experiences the difference between the world and his own ego"
(Steiner, 1924a/1982, p. 83). The separation of self from world which is
implied here is by no means a complete separation; rather, it corresponds in
large measure to Froebel's notion of the *reciprocity* of self and world described earlier. The child's ability to recognize and celebrate her newfound
autonomy is complemented and balanced by an ability to subtly preserve
the unity of selfhood and world.

This new relationship can best be characterized as a sort of rhythmic
give-and-take between child and world. It manifests itself in the games of
balance and skipping which children engage in during middle childhood,
but also in the rhythmic wordplay and oral incantations which often accom-
pany such games. On a physiological level, the rhythmic system finds its
clearest physical expression in the patterned movement of energy through
the child's body and conscious life, especially as manifested in the ceaseless
rhythm of pulse and breath:

> The thing of special importance for the second life period from the change of
> teeth to puberty is how the breathing process, with its rhythm, meets the blood
> circulation. This transformation of the forces taking place at the boundary
> between the breathing process and the circulatory blood system is of special
> importance . . . It is the balance, the harmonizing process between the blood
> system and the breathing system that is brought about in the period between
> the change of teeth and puberty. (Steiner, 1924b/1982, p. 58)

In the prenatal stage of growth, the syncopated rhythm of the heart
beats of mother and child imprinted a lifelong yearning for rhythm in the
preconscious memory of the unborn infant (Freeman, 1991). In her first
years of life, the young child established, with the support of her caregivers,
an equilibrium in the biological processes of life, in waking and sleeping,
feeding and eliminating, etc. In middle childhood, the rhythmic process
undergoes yet another transformation and begins to impress itself upon the
child's maturing conscious life. In their moral life, for example, many chil-

dren during this period exhibit a maturing sense of justice in their play activity with peers, built on a reciprocal notion of fairness and the need for rules. So too religious ceremonies and other ritualistic performances are entered into proudly and with the proper solemnity which they deserve.

For Steiner, the child's search for meaningfulness and purpose in the world is largely traceable to the rhythmic processes of middle childhood. In the same way that Froebel and Montessori traced this same function to the narrative mode, Steiner posited that the rhythmic processes of middle childhood are at the very heart of the child's search for meaningfulness, reciprocity, and continuity in the world. The rhythmic mode allows the child to perceive the world as an order-creating, patterned universe that celebrates diversity within the context of structured form. The child is equally attuned to patterns of integration (common forms and origins) and instances of differentiation (uniqueness and subjectivity). During middle childhood, the child exhibits a kind of "aesthetic comprehension" of the world rooted in the child's interior, emotional, and rhythmic life (Steiner, 1924a/1982, p. 66). The child's consciousness is caught somewhere between the imitative and immersive capacities of the younger child and the more mature, analytical consciousness of the adolescent.

Edith Cobb (1885–1977)

Among contemporary North American holistic theorists, one writer stands out, both as an inspiration to many and as a pioneer of holistic developmental thought in her own right. Published in 1977, only a few months after her death and following a lifetime of study and observation of children, *The Ecology of Imagination in Childhood* is Edith Cobb's testament to her quest to uncover what she described as the "genius of childhood."

Born into an upper-middle-class family in New York, Cobb spent much of her adult life serving on the boards of various charities and social agencies. Late in life, Cobb decided on a career in social work. Following her graduation from Columbia University in 1948, she began a personal search for the roots of genius in the autobiographies of childhood. Over the next several decades she would amass several hundred volumes of childhood autobiographies (today stored at the Teachers College Library at Columbia University) and integrate her discoveries with the psychological and cultural anthropological findings of the day.

Cobb's prose integrated scientific thought and poetry in a manner that echoed similar efforts by Rudolf Steiner to bring the scientific and artistic communities closer together. Her thesis—that the spontaneously creative imagination of childhood is integral to mental health in adulthood—focused particularly on middle childhood as a pivotal period of development.

"It occurred to me," Cobb wrote of this period (1977, p. 16), "that child and nature were engaged in some corresponding bioaesthetic striving fundamental to the fulfillment of individual human biological development." In an earlier paper (1969), she outlined her thesis as follows:

> My position is based upon the fact that the study of the child in nature, culture, and society . . . reveals that there is a special period, the little-understood, prepubertal, halcyon, middle age of childhood, approximately from five or six to eleven or twelve — between the strivings of animal infancy and the storm of adolescence — when the natural world is experienced in some highly evocative way, producing in the child a sense of some profound continuity with natural processes and presenting overt evidence of a biological basis of intuition. (pp. 123–124)

Early in her book Cobb distinguishes between child and animal nature. Unlike other animal species, the human child displays a "spontaneous striving to go beyond biological fulfillment . . . to add form and novelty to the environment" (1977, p. 15). Cobb relates such a striving to nature's inexorable and creative drive toward speciation and novelty through evolution. Development in childhood is not simply a growth phenomenon, but also a form of evolutionary striving. The strivings of the child are a microcosm reflection of the same drive towards form-creating experimentation in nature.

"Every child tries to structure a world," Cobb wrote (p. 17), and it is the child's plasticity of response to the world which is the epigenesis both of later development, but also the child's more immediate desire to "create in order to learn and know" (p. 24). At the root of the child's world-making is a capacity for wonder. For Cobb, wonder in childhood entails both "novelty of experience," but also an "expectancy of fulfillment" (p. 28). In the first view, wonder is an attraction to the unexplored. In the second, it is the promise of "more to come" or "better still, 'more to do'" (p. 28), which is aroused in the child by the mystery of some external stimulus that the child feels compelled to know.

To the child, the world reveals not only its mystery, but also its lawfulness. Learning that one may make use of this lawfulness is an important lesson of childhood. It also underscores the reflexive, even dialectical, nature of the relationship between self and world. Cobb regarded the child's relationship to nature as a kind of mutual engagement or interplay between child and world, as an "adaptive give-and-take between living organisms and their environments" (p. 29). She wrote that for the young child,

> the eternal questioning of the nature of the real is largely a wordless dialectic between self and world. When language renders this confrontation articulate,

it becomes an undertone to all persistent questioning by the child. The adult who senses this need and responds with integrity to the child's inquiries will find the child's heart and mind linked with his own. (pp. 31–32)

For Cobb, the development of language is not simply an exercise in communicative competence. As an instrument of exploration, language also provides the means by which the child can structure a world. Through exercises in taxonomy, the child learns to classify experience and the objects around her. To this spatial representation of the universe, add the dimension of time which introduces a new level of complexity into the child's world-making. "To be meaningful," wrote Cobb (p. 48), "the dimension of time must achieve expression in some pattern." In childhood, time is given continuity and patterned form through story. Here, argued Cobb, are the roots of the rhythmic foundation of middle childhood. Time and growth are linked together in a continuous narrative which unfolds as the child "moves forward from unstructured form into a theory of the universe" (p. 51):

> In childhood, the cognitive process is essentially poetic because it is lyrical, rhythmic, and formative in a generative sense; it is a sensory integration of self and environment . . . the child "knows" or re-cognizes [sic] in these moments that he makes his own world and that his body is a unique instrument, where the powers of nature and human nature meet. (p. 89)

In an analysis of her extensive collection of childhood autobiographies, Cobb found that many of her subjects (mainly artists and other creative thinkers) reported having some form of intuitive peak experience in childhood, often centered around an "acute sensory response to the natural world" (p. 30). As an example, she quoted Bernard Berenson's recollection of a peak experience which occurred when he was around six years old:

> As I look back on fully seventy years of awareness and recall the moments of greatest happiness, they were for the most part moments when I lost myself all but completely in some instant of perfect harmony . . . In childhood and boyhood this ecstasy overtook me when I was happy out of doors. Was I five or six? Certainly not seven. It was a morning in early summer. A silver haze shimmered and trembled over the lime trees. The air was laden with their fragrance. The temperature was like a caress. I remember—I need not recall— that I climbed up a tree stump and felt suddenly immersed in Itness. I did not call it by that name. I had no need for words. It and I were one. (p. 32)

In Berenson's case, as in other similar examples cited by Cobb [as well as Edward Robinson (1977) and Thomas Armstrong (1985)] the child seems to be momentarily immersed in some preverbal and transpersonal engagement with nature that invokes the child's perceptual participation with the cosmos as a whole. "The exaltation that the child feels," Cobb argued, "is a passionate response to an awareness of his own psychophysical growth potential as a continuity of nature's behavior" (p. 33). She commented further that

> in these memories the child appears to have experienced both a momentary sense of discontinuity — an awareness of his unique separateness and identity — and a revelatory sense of continuity — an immersion of his whole organism in the outer world of forms, colors, and motions in unparticularized time and space. This type of apprehension is certainly not intellectual. It is often mistakenly thought to be either mystical or tally subject and irrational; I suggest that it is rational, at least in a limited sense, as a preverbal experience of an aesthetic logic present in both nature's formative process and the gestalt-making powers and sensibilities of the child's own developing nervous system. (p. 88)

Cobb was sensitive to the fact that the peak experiences recollected by her subjects might not necessarily be reported by all children.[3] Fearing that some readers may judge her interpretation of childhood to be too mystical, Cobb instead emphasized its affective quality and the celebratory nature of the child's world-making over other more spiritual explanations. The child's continuity with nature, she argued, is "basically aesthetic and infused with joy in the power to know and to be" (p. 23). It is unassuming by its very nature, which gives it its enchanting quality.

A number of contemporary theorists have been greatly influenced by Edith Cobb's view of childhood. Among them is Paul Shepard, who included Cobb's original essay in his coedited book *The subversive science: Essays toward an ecology of man* (1969). Next we turn to Shepard's conception of middle childhood.

Paul Shepard (1925–1996)

Paul Shepard's view of childhood arose not from a psychological or educational standpoint, as is the case with the developmental theories reviewed above, but rather from the perspective of a cultural historian. His basic argument was that our modern day alienation from the natural world has resulted in stunted human development — the "disablement of ontogeny" (1982, p. ix). This estrangement of the human from the natural world has, in his view, led to a kind of psychological retardation in humans. Shepard traced the origins of this impasse to the Agricultural Revolution in Western civilization. He followed the increased domestication of animals during this period, as well as the stepped-up reliance on hierarchical and authoritarian forms of social control and the rise of mechanistic ways of thinking, through to the Reformation, and finally to present day society. His thesis was that infants and children historically enjoyed an intimate and special connection to the natural world (in Paleolithic cultures), but that this connection has been strained in recent centuries through our continuing efforts to dislodge and shelter the human species from an interdependent relationship with the balance of nature.

Shepard's view of childhood recognized clear signposts on the road to maturity so that the individual is seen to emerge "in a genetic calendar by stages, with time-critical constraints and needs, so that instinct and experience act in concert . . . resonating between disjunction and unity" (1982, p. 109). For Shepard, such stages entailed "likeness but difference" (p. 10). They were marked both by a series of separations—as the child matures from the subjective oneness of prenatal life to a clear sense of her own uniqueness and identity—but also by a sense of continuity with nature as process. In this way, argued Shepard (p. 14), the path towards maturity manifests itself both as "a growing sense of the separateness of the self" as well as "kinship to the Other . . . defined by a web of relationship and metaphorical common ground." Shepard's model of development represents this ebb and flow not as linear line of development (i.e., straight up), but as a spiral that "resonates between disjunction and unity . . . separation and symbioses" (p. 109).

It is during the first few months of life, in an effort to localize the sources of stimuli (i.e., to separate "I" from "not-I"), that the initial separations occur as the child first comes to know the world through his experience of taste and touch. Gradually, through interaction with self and mother, a "body schema" unfolds which lays the groundwork for the child's development of self-concept. By the age of four, the child has embarked on a new phase of growth. "Behind him," wrote Shepard (1973),

> is the experience of unity with the amniotic pond, which all his life will be the foundation of his security as a living organism. As an infant he has drawn the first rough drafts of body awareness and ego by using his muscles and senses to locate himself relative to and apart from objects. Touch and taste have linked his earliest memory to motion. All later learning will also bear the stamp of this relationship. (p. 187)

Next to the acquisition of language, play serves as the most fundamental organizing activity of the child's world. "Like language-learning," Shepard wrote (p. 199), "play is programmed in the human genes and its developmental expression is age-critical. It is essential for the growth of mental life." Through fantasy play, the child "creates a meaningful whole . . . [as] he and his companions build skeleton dramas of life, or 'plays,' which have continuity and cause and effect . . . Here the mind's journey begins" (p. 198). Shepard distinguished between several varieties of play:

> There is solitary play, play with objects, and play with others. There is primate-herbivore play [swinging, hanging, climbing, tumbling, sliding, and wrestling] . . . and there is (a little later, usually) carnivore play [stalking, rushing, hiding, creeping, chasing, eluding, attacking, and yielding]. There is investigative, exploratory play, which carries the young away from [the] mother, and affectionate play, which enhances the bond to her. There is play in collecting and making things, and finally there are games, or ritualized play. (p. 196)

The play experiences of children not only spur on social growth and development. They also provide children with the opportunity to "play out" ritualized roles and sequences of events in repeated form. Most essential about play, argues Shepard, are the "patterns" of play — the rule-making, and struggle for form — not solely the play activity itself. "The hunger for constant themes" is what play provides for, and this is an "age-group need [which] is part of the construction of a coherent and predictable world" (p. 199).

During middle childhood, ritualized play often manifests itself in gang-like activities complete with secret hideaways, clubhouses, and forts. Here the spirit of play and place are bound up together in a unique fantasy world of secrecy, adventure, and challenge. The cross-cultural preoccupation of both boys and girls with secret meeting places, forts, and other "favorite places" (Sobel, 1993) — both "discovered" and built by children — led Shepard (1977) to conclude that like play, place "is structured differently in juvenile life than at later ages; it is much more critically defined. It is intensely concerned with paths and boundaries, with hiding places and other special places for particular things" (p. 8). In middle childhood, such juvenile play space is configured in its membership to both purposefully include and exclude, to provide "retreat, solitude, and disengagement" (p. 8) for the lucky few:

> In these special places which he will always remember with peculiar reverence, the child's play is at once monkey- and cat-like. It is hiding, stalking, and capture. Pursuit, flight, scuffling, and organizing are woven through secret hideaways, cherished trees or thickets, rock piles or dumps, basements and alleys. Venturing, concealment, and retreat are intensely suspenseful and emotional . . . The landscape to the child is animated . . . The rhythm of being with and being apart from, coming and going, joining and separation in games is a dynamic recognition of the livingness of nature. (Shepard, 1967, p. 35)

In Shepard's view, the natural landscape of the play environment mirrors the emerging mental landscape of the mind of the child. A vibrant, richly textured play space is equated with a thriving mental life, and a barren, stagnant play space, devoid of natural context, with the psychological retardation of mental growth. The critical importance of "place" in childhood leads Shepard to postulate that the child has three ecological needs through early and middle childhood which are intrinsically related to the quality of his interactions with the natural world. These include

> architecturally complex play space shared with companions; a cumulative and increasingly diverse experience of non-human forms, animate and inanimate, whose taxonomic names and generic relationships he must learn; and occasional and progressively more strenuous excursions into the wild world where he may, in a limited way, confront the non-human. (1973, p. 267)

As with Cobb, Shepard firmly believed that the natural world holds certain inner secrets that the child yearns to discover. "The child learns that all life tells [him] something," wrote Shepard (1982, p. 11), "and that all sound—from the frog calling to the sea surf—issues from a being kindred and significant to himself, telling some tale, giving some clue, mimicking some rhythm that he should know." Of special significance to Shepard was the young child's fascination with animals, reflected both in the imitative patterns of their play and through the anthropomorphic character of their dreams (Pearce, 1992). "Animals have a magnetic affinity for the child," noted Shepard (1982, p. 7), "for each seems to embody some impulse, reaction, or movement that is 'like me.'"

PARADIGMS OF GROWTH: AN INTERPRETIVE
VIEW OF DEVELOPMENT IN CHILDHOOD

The preceding accounts of middle childhood point to the potentially pivotal role played by the natural world, story, rhythm, and place in informing the child's emerging cosmology of the universe. Each account has been chosen—despite even major variations in interpretation—because it delineates a functional vision of development in childhood, a vision that is congruent with the recovery of the ecological imperative in contemporary society. For each theorist, it is the unity of selfhood and world, between the ages of about six and twelve, which establishes middle childhood as the sensitive period for the acquisition of an ecologically sensitive cosmology of the world. The child's affinity for the world is characterized as a sort of rhythmic "give-and-take" between child and world, a kind of mutual engagement or interplay between self and nature and the physical and cultural worlds which surround the child. During middle childhood, there is an expressed effort on the part of the child to exercise new modes of thought, to search for the causes of things, and to establish a personal history for oneself. Middle childhood builds upon the child's primary powers of perception and further refines her sense of self—not in isolation from the world—but in relationship to its nurturing capacities and the diversity of experiences which it affords. As such a period comprises nothing less than a full-scale cultural reworking of the human organism through childhood, perhaps it finds its most basic roots in the movement of energy through time.

The most striking manifestation of motion in the human organism is the respiratory process which functions as the organic center of our existence literally from our first breath to our last. (Respiration is also our a priori connection to the earth all through life.) With the first intake of air into our lungs, the regulatory capacity of the respiratory process is engaged. Respiration serves as an effective metaphor for the patterned movement of energy in early and middle childhood, for in the groping stage of infancy, breathing is irregular and weak, but it gradually grows stronger and steadier in order to provide the rhythmic foundation for middle childhood.

In childhood, motion is both internally and externally regulated. Growth forces work inwardly on the organism of the young child and on a structural and organic level inform her developing consciousness. In the fetal stage and in infancy, these growth forces are engaged in a massive physical (re)structuring of the human body so that this early period of growth functions as nothing less than the total activation and release of the most formative of biological energies on the child's organism. Through cellular regeneration the body reconstructs itself during its first years of existence. The completion of this reconstruction is heralded by the changing of the milk teeth, which also signals a universally recognized shift to a new life epoch around age six. The biological foundation of development is now secure and the child begins to attend to the physical and cultural worlds surrounding her on an increasingly conscious level.

The young child's relatedness to the world is of a different quality than that to be found in either middle childhood or adolescence. It is suggested that three modes of relatedness—here termed *mastery, immersion,* and *engagement*—find their expression at different stages in the child's development (see Figure 4.1). These faculties tell us something of how the child relates to the world as she matures. The mastery orientation points to specific milestones and achievements on the road to adulthood, and the immersion orientation to a "subjective oneness" with the world in infancy and early childhood. The mode of engagement rests in between these two orientations, and, emerging in middle childhood, highlights the child's ca-

Figure 4.1. Developmental Patterns of Differentiation and Integration

Adulthood

"Tests of Proficiency"   Adolescence   "Self-as-Kingroup"

Mastery   Immersion

Middle Childhood

"Reciprocity of Self and World"
"Building a Functional Cosmology of the Universe"

Engagement

Mastery   Immersion

"Meeting the   "Self-as-Cosmos"
Challenges of
Nature"
                        Infancy and
                        Early Childhood

pacity to further refine her sense of self while subtly preserving the unity of selfhood and world. In charting the child's growth from infancy to the emergence of the narrative mode in middle childhood, this chapter concludes by considering how a reevaluation of each of these three orientations might contribute to a new interpretative view of childhood which takes as its cue the reciprocal nature of the child's changing relationship to the natural world and the physical and cultural worlds which surround the child.

In the last chapter, it was argued that our modern-day story of development in childhood generally recognizes only the progressive element in the design of childhood to the detriment of other possibilities for relatedness. A "line of development," perhaps not unlike the trajectory of an airplane taking off, could be indicated to depict the child's growth from incompleteness to completeness. Such a line is primarily one of *mastery*, of learning to overcome and manipulate one's immediate (and later, not so immediate) environments. If we placed an equal emphasis on the capacity for immersion and engagement, that line would likely be one of a different sort, perhaps best represented in the form of a circle, helix, various intersecting planes, or otherwise.

To be sure, a mastery element is itself integral to the design of a childhood, so that failure to engage this capacity would also mean failure to overcome (i.e., meet the challenges of) earthly forces, which is a primary developmental task of infancy and early childhood. As these forces are essentially primal by nature, as in the case of the ceaseless pull of gravity on the child or the unrelenting appeal of a rich symbolic universe that the child feels compelled to know, each must be squarely reckoned with in its own right. The strivings of the child and the fruits of her labor lead to a mastery of these forces as embodied by the two fundamental tasks of early childhood—walking and talking.

Nature's forces challenge and impinge upon the child's earliest efforts to make her way in the world, but the child [perhaps unconsciously expectant of the creative (and cultural) energies to soon be released in middle childhood] finds the means by which to counter these forces within the strivings of her *will*ful drive toward biological self-fulfillment. Perhaps we can expect the child's willfulness and persistence, which is evident until about age four or five, never again to reach this same intensity unless her very survival and birthright are at stake once more. Witness the cry of the newborn in a strange land, or the resolve of the 4-year-old holding a favorite cereal in a supermarket. The child's will, her striving for self-fulfillment, is indiscriminate and often overbearing, yet quite possibly integral to nature's plan for ensuring her physical and emotional survival during these first sensitive years.

Significantly, it is not enough to point exclusively to the mastery element as the only line of development in childhood, for it is precisely a sole reliance on this capacity that could potentially leave us without the ability to envision and transform our relationship with the wider earth community into one of a more harmonious and sustainable kind. Therefore, in addition to the mastery orientation, it is suggested that we find in childhood two alternative modes of interaction with the world. The first of these modes emerges parallel to the mastery orientation and is the young child's capacity for *immersion* into her immediate surroundings. The second mode of engagement follows later in middle childhood.

What is meant here by a capacity for immersion? Fundamentally, this faculty entails an intimacy between self and world, i.e., with that which exists beyond the boundaries of one's own body, so that *self* essentially becomes embodied by *world*. The child becomes earthbound in the most marked of senses, richly rewarded by a multitude of tantalizing sensations, cherished tastes, and treasured observations that are fed into the little child's organism for her to savor. Witness the small child's enchantment with her food, how her fantasy experience can be enticed by a single object for hours at a time, or how a mud puddle is met with a whole afternoon's rapture. Here perhaps lies the richness of early childhood in its deepest essence, the inspiration for countless poets and painters through history, and the ideal model for a renewed communion with the earth. The young child enters deeply into the structure of her world and just as deeply allows this world to enter into her. In this way the entire organism of the little child, up to about age 3 or 4, functions as a giant sense organ, as it were, in a kind of "participation mystique" with the world, to use Jung's phrase.

> *There was a child went forth every day,*
> *and the first object he looked upon,*
> *that object he became.*
>
> *And that object became part of him for the day*
> *or a certain part of the day,*
> *or for many years or stretching cycles of years . . .*
>
> —Walt Whitman (1961)

The young child's immersive relationship with the world is of a magical quality that is fundamentally estranged from the adult's experience of reality, but it is also a limited one in that the child can never quite fully recognize herself as being distinct and "functionally autonomous" from the world which exists beyond the boundaries of her little body. Never mind that a richer relationship with the world could never be found, or that we perhaps need go no further to discover a more authentic model of communion with the earth. The true essence of her humanity, her inherent destiny within the earth process, has not yet been realized. There are qualities of experience, nuances of reality yet to be discovered—new powers of cognition to be engaged. These new powers are the metacapacities of the older child and adult.

An initial awareness of these powers perhaps arises at the level of expectancy in the young child's vague notion of something beyond (and greater than) biological fulfillment. Her instinctive nature has taught her to imitate the behavior of those around her and this she does with the same faithfulness with which she allows the structure of her world to leave its multitude of impressions on her growing organism. But neither the faculty of imitation nor impressions left by the world can fully serve to promote her subjectivity, which is a necessary step in moving beyond biological fulfillment. This the child must do alone, and alone she does, around the age of two or three, through an original reference to herself in the first person. The child has first spoken of herself as "I."

On both literal and metaphorical levels, the significance of this event and the growth milestones leading up to and beyond it cannot be over-stated. This is a critical step in the child's existential awakening of selfhood. After this dawning of self, the immersive quality of the child's experiences can never be quite the same. She has eaten from the tree of knowledge, so to speak, and her awareness of this act has served to *separate* her from her participation mystique in life. Such a process of differentiation is one aspect of nature's plan for the young child, a preparation in fact for a new orientation to the world, and as such it will inevitably continue into middle childhood.

From her earliest years, the child has closely followed two contrasting modes of interaction with the world, in the form of a mastery and immersion orientation, but such a dichotomy of relatedness to the world is no longer sufficient to meet the strivings of the child's psychic energies toward actualization. It is suggested above that there are two monumental events which result in the mastery and immersion orientations becoming out-moded (at least for the present). First, the child has overcome the earthly forces which blocked the strivings of her willful drive toward biological self-fulfillment (i.e., she has a newfound mastery of mobility and language); and second, through an original reference to herself as "I," she has estab-lished herself (if only in a limited way) as distinct from the world. The child's need for a mastery orientation to the world is defunct because the biological basis of her existence is now secure. The child's capacity for immersion is defunct because she has taken the first step toward objectivity. Her quandary is that just at the moment she has secured the biological and human basis of her existence — and through this, set the stage for the further unfolding of her cultural life — she is faced with a dichotomy of relatedness to the world that undermines her strivings toward further development. This dichotomy must be resolved before the further unfolding of her cul-tural life can effectively take place. Nature paves the way to a resolution of this impasse with a new mode of relatedness to the world that spells that arrival of middle childhood and the emergence of the *engagement* orienta-tion in the child's relationship to the world. The dichotomy is effectively resolved.

OUR MODERN STORY of development in childhood has greatly devalued the role of middle childhood to the point where this period is often viewed as nothing more than a bridge between the more important chapters of early childhood and adolescence. More than that, middle childhood has traditionally been seen as a temporary reprieve from the fiery passions of early childhood and adolescence (witness the term *latency* which is so often attached to it) so that its vitality within the interplay of life is rarely revealed. Yet between the ages of about six and twelve we find the child searching for a functional cosmology of the universe and the fundamental task of middle childhood is to articulate such a cosmology in a formative way.

The child's inquiry into the universe functions as nothing less than a search for meaningfulness and purpose in the world of nature and in the physical and cultural worlds which surround the child. The child's striving toward cultural self-fulfillment presents itself as a celebratory response to his emerging selfhood and newfound mastery over earthly forces which marked his entry into middle childhood. As a period of youthful exuberance and mischievous adventures, middle childhood emerges as a celebratory response to the child's newfound powers over motion, balance, strength, and endurance. Each of these powers are further challenged by games of running, skipping, climbing, and balancing with the view of testing one's limits and "defying the odds."

Games of balance serve as tests of physical prowess, but balance is also significant as a guiding metaphor in the child's search for meaning, reciprocity, continuity, and form in the world of nature and the physical, cultural, and moral worlds that surround the child. Before this time, ensuring meaningfulness and purpose remained a primary responsibility of the young child's caregivers who maintained spatiotemporal regularity in his daily life and sought to ensure his participation in the rituals and community festivals which define the essence of the family and community to which he belongs. In general, meaningfulness and purpose were equated with satisfying intrapersonal security and belonging needs native to the young child's interaction with his immediate environments, but beginning in middle childhood, a *semantic* quality to the child's world-making begins to assert itself as he searches for the essential *quality of* and *meaning behind* those objects and events which he once took for granted in earlier childhood. During this period, language serves as the fundamental organizing activity of the child's world and provides the foundations for the symbolic manipulation of the inner, subjective and outer, intersubjective world of meanings.

A general timeline of utterances can be indicated for the child's mastery of speech. Development begins with the one-syllable primary sounds of early infancy; moves on to the metrical patterned speech of later infancy (comprising several primary sounds laced together, often in a singsong fashion); proceeds onward to the word combinations of early childhood where the *semantic* quality of speech makes its first appearance in the *thematic* sequencing of words; then continues on to longer and more complex word combinations and a maturing sense of the temporal essence of speech as evidenced through the use of tense.

The child's far-reaching command of language around age six is paralleled by and related to three pivotal events that have paved the way for a change in orientation to the world. First, as a consequence of the child's maturing sense of time (i.e., his emerging awareness of having a past and future), the child senses the first inklings of a need for a personal history. (Until only recently he has been absorbed in the spiritual reality of the moment, impervious to the flow of time from past to future.) Second, his mastery over language and mobility (and related gross and fine motor skills) and emerging awareness of self as distinct from the world have set the stage for the further unfolding of his cultural life and paved the way for him to co-construct and articulate an emerging functional cosmology of the universe. Finally, as discussed above, the child is faced with a dichotomy of relatedness to the world in the form of the two contrasting modes of mastery and immersion. It is under these conditions—the yearning for a personal history, a theory of the universe, and a new mode of relatedness to the world—that the narrative mode of inquiry native to middle childhood unfolds. In these intervening middle years between the struggle for biological self-fulfillment in early childhood and individual self-fulfillment in adolescence, the child embarks on a formative constructivist endeavor, aiming not only to build a functional cosmology of the universe, but also, to paraphrase Edith Cobb, a world in which to discover a self.

FROM THE EARLIEST moments of her life, and above all else, the child has placed her faith in a single quality of relatedness to the world. Her world has been built on trust—a trusting in the inherent goodness of caregivers and other adults, in the security of the world around her, and in the sanctity of the future. But with the completion of middle childhood, there arises deep within the early adolescent a need to nourish an independent line of thought and make an initial stand in the world on one's own terms and in one's own right. The arrival of adolescence is marked in part by a growing sense of discontinuity between the strivings of self, caregivers and the world at large, and a corresponding existential awakening to the darker (violent) powers at work in the universe as a whole.

One consequence of such an awakening may be a loss of implicit security in the adolescent's relationship to her caregivers and the world around her. This sense of loss is a natural consequence of growth and maturation into puberty. It manifests itself as a subtle if often momentary nuance within the private and psychological rite of passage from middle childhood to adolescence. Years later, in adulthood, perhaps during a quiet time of reflection or a moment of crisis, this sense of loss may resurface again as a fleeting desire to regain the implicit security and trust of early and middle childhood. But should this sense of loss remain unresolved by the early adolescent for too long, or be felt by the child too early, or at a level for which she is unprepared, the consequences for development can be profound.

The story of early and middle childhood, in all its various forms and manifestations, cannot be fully articulated without reference to the decisive effects that an erosion of trust and security will have on the child. Yet in the present chapter, and indeed, in most holistic and mainstream theories of development, a large measure of security in the child's interactions with her caregivers and world is an a priori assumption of growth in childhood. With the increased pressures of continued resource depletion and environmental degradation, not to mention a climate of inner city decay, street warfare, and seemingly rising levels of poverty and child abuse, such a measure of security cannot at present be assured or taken for granted. To help us appreciate more fully the decisive implications of such an erosion of trust and security, Chapter 5 turns to an exploration of dysfunctionality in the cultural construction of childhood and the role of danger in the lives of children.

CHAPTER 5

Childhood Trauma and Earth Crisis: Toward a Functional Vision of Childhood

If a child is to keep alive his inborn sense of wonder . . . he needs the companionship of at least one adult who can share it, rediscovering with him the joy, excitement, and mystery of the world we live in.
— Rachel Carson, *The Sense of Wonder* (1956/1990)

Despite enormous risks from their physical and social environment[s], most resilient children had the opportunity to establish a close bond with at least one person who provided them with stable care, so that they were able to develop a sense of basic trust . . . This person accepted them unconditionally, regardless of temperamental idiosyncrasies, physical attractiveness, or level of intelligence.
— James Garbarino et al., *Children in Danger* (1992)

One of the greatest challenges facing educators at present concerns the seemingly widening gulf between the idyllic kind of life which we would like to be able to guarantee to all children and the reality of life for many children who live in impoverished and violent communities around the world. While the scope of this book does not permit an exhaustive review of the impact of violence and poverty on the lives of children, it is appropriate to consider potential areas where holistic and ecologically sensitive reform efforts may overlap or run parallel to the efforts of researchers and practitioners whose daily work addresses the needs of children living in danger. If the apparent similarity of the two passages which begin this chapter is any indication — the first written within the context of the holistic tradition, the second from the perspective of children living amid social crisis — then such an exploration is more than warranted.

Chapter 4 closed with the observation that mainstream and holistic developmental theories have typically failed to account for the effects a loss of trust and security will have on development in childhood. In recognition of the likelihood that the environmental impasse we are now experiencing may soon strain many of the social supports afforded to children, we now address this concern, first by examining two examples of dysfunctionality in the cultural construction of childhood, and second by exploring the impact of community violence on the lives of children. At the close of this chapter, the discussion turns briefly to the potential impact environmental degradation and a declining resource base soon may have on the lives of U.S. and Canadian children.

Because the argument of this book hinges on the view that childhood is a distinct phase within the human life span with possibilities and constraints set apart from those of adulthood, it is necessary to counter the argument that differences between adults and children are largely minimal. The first part of this chapter aims to refute such a position. The discussion below situates childhood within the context of two contrasting examples of *dysfunctionality* in the cultural construction of childhood. It is argued that despite their obvious contradictions, the puritanical and liberationist conceptions of childhood share at least one element in common—both subscribe to an idea of the child in which inherent differences between children and adults are largely obscured.

DYSFUNCTIONALITY IN THE CULTURAL CONSTRUCTION OF CHILDHOOD

In Chapter 3, it was argued that the idea of the child, and especially religious ideals of the child as born inherently "good" or "evil," have strongly influenced the affectionate versus callous treatment of children throughout the modern period. In his review of the religious roots of violence against children in the Western world, Philip Greven (1991) gives a detailed account of the relationship between religious ideology and the patterned use of violence against children. Throughout the modern era, the use of corporal punishment has largely been ideologically justified and perpetuated via the underlying religious and social visions of the time. Although Greven's argument is largely concerned with how this process has unfolded throughout history, he also points out that many of these notions of the subjugation of the child still find expression in society at present and not-so-subtly influence contemporary patterns of child rearing within many cultures. The passage by La Haye below, published in a 1977 child-rearing manual, represents (one hopes) an extreme example of such a position:

> Your child's desire for evil can be related to the weaknesses of his temperament while his desire for good can be seen in the strengths of his temperament. It is

of great benefit to the parent when he realizes that it is natural for his child to have a desire for evil. The child is not just being obstinate and uncooperative but is following that natural desire to learn more about and to experience *evil*. There is a conflict going on within him because he has not yet been quickened or alerted to spiritual values. He is born with very selfish desires and thinks only of his own wants. When denied his wants, he reacts with rage and fits of anger. Can you see what a teenager or an adult would be like if left to those natural ego-centered desires? (p. 3, emphasis in original)

The author is clearly working within a fundamentalist context and elsewhere uses direct quotations from the Bible to validate her thesis that the child has a desire for evil. She praises parents for recognizing such desires and reassures them that they have chosen the proper context within which to view their children's behavior. So too the element of fear is strategically used here to raise doubts in parents' minds about the consequences of more lenient approaches to discipline. Finally, the author shows a total lack of understanding for those natural maturational processes that will gradually lead the child from self-centeredness into adult behavioral patterns.

Perhaps the most dangerous element of such advice is the extent to which the author has attempted to mask differences in inherent levels of power between the adult and child. Here the child is viewed as being on par with the adult, his egoism a real and significant threat to the adult's authority. Adult notions of selfishness are projected onto even the youngest child, who is despised for thinking only of his own wants. Contempt becomes the defining criterion upon which the behavior of the child is to be judged and leads to harsh and deceptive prescriptions for his treatment:

There are right and wrong spankings. A wrong spanking would be a cruel, sadistic beating that is given in rage. This causes a child is be filled with anger and revenge and has not benefited him. A right spanking is given with a sound, positive approach. First, there needs to be communication on why the spanking will be given, and then it should be with a "rod" of correction and much love. One father had a paddle made with these words inscribed: "To my son with love." (La Haye, 1977, p. 145)

Whether delivered as a "cruel, sadistic beating" or in a "sound, positive" manner, the consequences of violent treatment go far beyond the resulting immediate and physical harm to the child.[1] Children are also damaged psychologically by such treatment—especially when they are made to show gratitude for the violence which is inflicted upon them (as is likely in the above example). Also, there can be severe developmental consequences to such treatment, consequences which perhaps manifest themselves, years later, in adulthood. Alice Miller (1984a), a Swiss psycho-therapist, proposes the following developmental theory to account for the implications of the violent and exploitive treatment of children. She argues that the individual psychological stages in the lives of abused children are:

1. To be hurt as a small child without anyone recognizing the situation as such.
2. To fail to react to the suffering with anger.
3. To show gratitude for what are supposed to be good intentions.
4. To forget [repress] everything.
5. To discharge the stored-up anger onto others in adulthood or to direct it against oneself. (p. 106)

Despite its religious roots, the account described above does not pre-clude the positive role religion can play in the upbringing of children. Child rearing within a Christian or any other religious/spiritual tradition clearly *can* provide a secure and meaningful environment for growth when such traditions emphasize a compassionate and supportive caregiving role for adults. The danger arises when the authority of religion (or any other ideology) is coopted and used to mask and substantiate the violent and exploitive treatment of children. As we move forward to reengage those spiritual traditions which support the recovery of sustainable relations with the natural world, we need to be especially wary of historic precedents in certain puritanical and other nonsectarian reactionary prescriptions for the treatment of children. These precedents (judging from the book cited above) still make their impact today and could potentially intensify as the plight of the human becomes increasingly precarious in the face of dramatic environmental change.

The subjugation of the child advocated by the above example repre-sents an extreme position in the debate over child rearing practices. At the opposite end of the spectrum, the child liberationist movement calls for the emancipation of children from a subservient position within society. Work-ing from a conceptual context not unlike that presented in Chapter 3, the liberationist movement regards powerlessness in childhood to be culturally constructed (rather than biologically constructed) and a function of inequal-ity in the social freedoms extended to children (as compared with those extended to adults). Arguing from an equal rights perspective, R. G. Des Dixon (1992) outlines the basic position of the child liberationist movement in this way:

The principle must be that every individual has complete rights from concep-tion (or birth or some point in between if pro-abortion factions prevail). It is the responsibility of society to protect those rights until each individual chooses to exercise them. Each individual will begin to exercise various rights according to his or her own developmental timetable and needs; but generally, at puberty, every individual can be expected to exercise all rights personally, with or without benefit of counsel, whichever he/she chooses. Any individual may elect to exercise rights personally before puberty or may choose not to exercise rights after puberty. (p. 199)

From the liberationist perspective, the child's participation in society, including her place of residence, required attendance at school, affiliations, and choices in companionship are all judged to be unduly limited by severe restrictions on the child's movements and activities. The child holds relatively little economic power and what little she does have is administered by and through her parents and other adults. In cases where her rights are violated, the child does not always hold the same legal status or recourse as adults. As a consequence, she is often subject to separate statutes and measures in the eyes of the law. Add to this the fact that the child holds few political rights and it is clear that gross social inequalities permeate every aspect of the child's life. The solution, argue child liberationists, is to extend to children *all* of the same rights and privileges which adults currently take for granted. In this way, unnecessary distinctions between children and adults will gradually erode, and all persons regardless of age will be conceived of in the same way and offered similar levels of support from social institutions.

In the above passage, Dixon's position represents a moderate stand within the child liberationist movement in that he (at least) acknowledges that there is a "developmental timetable" in children's maturation into adulthood which could potentially affect children's abilities to exercise equal rights. In other liberationist accounts (e.g., Farson, 1974) such a developmental vision of childhood remains largely unacknowledged. Yet even in Dixon's account the distinction between children and adults is mute at best, since even the youngest preadolescent is judged ready to make a rational decision for herself regarding her ability to exercise her rights effectively.

Although no culture-wide experiments that aim to evaluate child liberationist proposals have ever been attempted, psychological research into the effects of permissive parenting practices roughly correspond to the liberationist vision of a "liberated" household and show that children who are largely left to their own devices, without adult direction, mostly face negative developmental outcomes from such neglect. Laura M. Purdy (1992), in her critique of the liberationist position, draws the following conclusions in reviewing several such studies which explore the effects of various parenting practices on children:

In general, the picture [that emerges] here associates impulsiveness, irresponsibility, disorganization, aggression, and general immaturity with laissez-faire permissiveness. Conversely, democratic permissiveness that is characterized by some kind of high control, coupled with rational explanation and warmth, is related to the opposite traits. These studies are remarkably consistent, given the difficulties inherent to such work; there appears to be no solid evidence refuting them. (pp. 105–106)

In sharp contrast to the liberationist view that differences between adults and children are largely culturally constructed, and despite the argument presented in Chapter 3 (which, if carried to its logical consequences, could also be related to such a view), it is argued here that there are certain *inherent* differences between children and adults which cannot be eradicated by way of even the most carefully crafted social reform agenda. An extended period of neoteny in the human species implies that children, regardless of cultural context, mature gradually over a period of several years and do not yet have recourse to the same inherent abilities as adults. As James Garbarino and his associates (1992) write in relation to children's susceptibility to danger,

Young children are more vulnerable. Their physical immaturity places them at risk for injury from trauma that would not hurt adults because they are larger and more powerful. Their psychic immaturity means they are more easily shocked by the awful things that adults have grown accustomed to know about. (p. 5)

This passage points to two fundamental differences between adults and children which pervade every context of the child's life, and, contrary to the arguments put forth by liberationist theorists, remain constant regardless of the cultural context and in spite of social reform agendas. These conditions are the context within which all primary relationships with adults are played out in early and middle childhood, even insofar as such conditions remain unacknowledged and unaddressed within the cultural construction of childhood.

First, children are *physically* less powerful than adults. Until early to mid-adolescence, most children are smaller and weaker than adults. Because they are still maturing, children's bone structure, muscles, and other tissues are less well formed (Tanner, 1978). Beyond issues of size, weight, and strength, however, are other physiological differences. For example, children require greater amounts of sleep than do most adults, and for all children the regulation of physiological functioning emerges as a major goal of early childhood.

Second, children are *psychologically* less powerful than adults. More precisely, children are psychologically dependent on adults for care and support all through childhood. Although the kind of care and support required by children beyond early childhood may be of a different quality, as peers gradually come to play an increasingly significant role in children's lives for example, psychological dependency on adults is never totally dissipated until at least mid-adolescence (and often later, in many societies). Particularly for children who are living under extreme duress (e.g., who are victims of community violence), research has shown that the strength of the parent–child relationship is a better indicator of the child's psychological health than the scale of the community violence itself (Garbarino, 1992). On a somewhat more subtle level, the adult's mediation of the child's psychological life is likely a primary indicator of healthy psychological growth into adulthood regardless of the social context.

Clearly evident within most liberationist accounts is a failure to address the above characteristics of childhood which define early development as a unique and vulnerable phase within the human life cycle deserving of greater protective status than that afforded to adults. To admit to differences in adult and child functioning — differences which largely rest on inequitable levels of *inherent* power rather than *social* power and therefore cannot be remedied at the level of social reform — would do serious damage to the case for equal rights for children. The irony may be that in failing to address the unique qualities of childhood, liberationist theorists put forward a conception of childhood that is fundamentally adult-centered and at odds with the important efforts that can be made on behalf of children at present.

At their most fundamental level, the puritanical and liberationist visions of childhood would seem to be juxtaposed to each other and virtually irreconcilable. Yet both forward a view of childhood in which inherent differences between adults and children are largely minimized. In the case of the first view, differences in inherent levels of power between adults and children are obscured, which provides the ideological justification for the brutal treatment of children advocated by the puritanical position. In the case of the liberationist view, differences in inherent levels of functioning between adults and children are judged to be minimal, which provides the ideological justification for eroding the sources of support required by children for healthy development into adulthood. In failing to recognize childhood as a unique and vulnerable phase within the human life span, both traditions forward a vision of childhood which is fundamentally dysfunctional and estranged from the most basic primary care needs of children. Such an analysis would seem to indicate that holding a conception of childhood in which certain inherent differences between children and adults are recognized (and legitimated) may be integral to constructions of childhood in which the physical and psychosocial needs of children are met. If so, eroding such distinctions would represent the first step in the move away from functionality in the cultural construction of childhood. Valerie Polakow (1992) underscores the point in this way:

> It is only when we develop a separate image of childhood as a distinctive ontological state that we begin to propound a differential morality that recognizes the special vulnerabilities and needs of the infant and child. (pp. 5–6)

This discussion points to the pivotal role that dysfunctionality in the "idea of the child" can play in eroding social supports for children. However, the idea of the child represents only one of several factors which can impact negatively on children's lives. For reasons other than mere ideological constructions of childhood, many children living in North America and elsewhere around the world also lack the opportunity of growing up with the support and care needed from adult caregivers and the wider community. Therefore it is also important to consider the impact of various other social conditions on the lives of children, perhaps especially the role played by violence in disrupting children's lives. The discussion below moves on to explore the seemingly increasing role of danger in the lives of children, focusing particularly on the role of community violence in disrupting healthy development in childhood.

THE DEVELOPMENTAL TOLL OF LIVING IN DANGER

James Garbarino and his associates (1992) have studied the effects of community violence on children living in North America and various other areas of the world, including Mozambique, Nicaragua, Cambodia, and the Middle East. They cite the following case example to illustrate the multifaceted consequences for children living in danger in the United States:

> Robert is four years old. He lives in a public housing project in Chicago. His ten-year-old sister was raped last month by a teenager in the building. His fifteen-year-old cousin was killed in a gang shoot-out last year. His mother's current boyfriend used to beat him and his sister when they misbehaved, until his sixteen-year-old brother and his gang threatened to kill him if he continued hitting the younger children. Recently, Robert's brother was arrested on charges that included drug dealing and assault with a deadly weapon. Now he can no longer help out financially or offer his protection. Such is Robert's complex connection with "community violence." Among Robert's classmates at school, Anna saw her brother shot on the street. Jose's arm was broken by

his stepfather. Anita was trapped on the playground when a gang shoot-out started. (p. xii)

Children living in the midst of urban violence are both the intended and unintended victims of stray bullets, drive-by shootings, beatings, stabbings, and associated gang violence. They are witnesses to violence, and their parents, brothers, sisters, and friends are often its victims. Many children are also financially and/or psychologically dependent on the perpetrators of violence. Gang members are older brothers, sisters' boyfriends, and idolized neighbors. Garbarino and his associates (1992) cite estimates that by age 5, most children living in the poorest inner-city neighborhoods of U.S. cities have had some kind of firsthand encounter with shootings and by adolescence, fully one-third have been witnesses to homicides.

Approaching childhood from a developmental perspective means recognizing that the effects of community violence on children are likely to be different than the effects of the same violence on adults. Age and developmental level largely influence how children react to violence and interpret the danger around them (Garbarino et al., 1992). Young children tend to display passive reactions to violence and exhibit regressive behaviors such as bedwetting and clinging behavior. In middle childhood, children may exhibit increased aggressive tendencies, develop somatic complaints, and experience serious learning and behavioral difficulties in school. By the time of puberty, aggressive impulses may manifest themselves in the form of delinquent or self-destructive behavior and the adolescent may experience serious problems in forming a stable identity.

The number of risk factors facing children can also affect their ability to cope with chronic trauma. Children who are victims of community violence are also likely to be victims of poverty, are more likely to be malnourished, and may be coping with other stressful conditions in their lives (e.g., inadequate housing and family violence). In the United States, children under the age of 6 are more likely to be living in poverty than children in any other age group (National Center for Children in Poverty, 1990), and there is little indication that conditions are improving. For example, between 1968 and 1987, the number of American children living in poverty increased by 35%, and in 1990 families with children represented about one-third of the total homeless population in the United States.

THE ROLE OF THE CARING ADULT IN THE LIFE OF THE CHILD

Research studies that address the impact of community violence and other stressful events on the lives of children have matured from an exclusive focus on the negative developmental outcomes of this violence to an exploration of those specific factors which can best help children to cope with crisis and survive emotionally in the long term. In the more recent literature, the concepts of *resiliency* and *protective factors* have been used to account for how some children are able to emerge relatively intact emotionally and psychologically despite the hardships they face (Werner, 1990). Researchers use the term resiliency to refer to those intrinsic characteristics of the individual child which help the child to adapt successfully to and cope with stressful life events. Essentially, resiliency refers to specific components of a person's character, such as a high level of sociability or a feeling of self-competence, which can serve as a buffer of resistance to hardship and suffering. These internal characteristics of the individual are further supported by various protective factors related to surrounding environmental and social conditions such as support from social institutions, family members, and other caregivers.

In a cross-cultural review of the literature on the roots of resiliency in childhood and adolescence, Emmy E. Werner (1990) identified specific characteristics of resilient children at various stages of life. During infancy, resilient children exhibit "predictable temperamental characteristics that elicit positive responses" (p. 100) from others. To their caregivers they appear active, affectionate, and easy to deal with. Through early childhood, resilient children display "a pronounced sense of autonomy and social orientation" (p. 101) that derives from "a coping pattern that combines autonomy (i.e., an ability to provide their own structure) with an ability to ask for support when [it is] needed" (p. 103). During middle childhood, resilient children exhibit an enhanced sense of self-competence, and both boys and girls display a high degree of autonomy and independence, as well as a capacity for nurturance and emotional expressiveness. Finally, in adolescence, resilient youth exhibit a "pronounced social maturity and strong sense of responsibility" (p. 194), as well as a high sense of self-efficacy, a belief that even when confronted with great hardship, they can nevertheless overcome the obstacles that they face and exert considerable control over their future.

Depending on the nature and severity of the conflict surrounding them, possessing some or all of the above characteristics may be a necessary but insufficient precondition for children's psychological survival into adulthood. Werner also notes a number of additional protective factors which can contribute to resiliency in childhood. These include the supportive role played by siblings and other family members, compassionate but firm child-rearing practices, and a community environment that imbues a strong sense of meaningfulness and purpose:

A number of studies of resilient children from a wide variety of socioeconomic and ethnic backgrounds have noted that their families have held religious

beliefs that provided stability and meaning to their lives, especially in times of
hardship and adversity. The content of their faith varied from Buddhism to
Mormonism to Catholicism and fundamental and liberal versions of Protes-
tantism and Judaism. What such faiths appear to give resilient children and
their caregivers is a sense of rootedness and coherence, a conviction that their
lives have meaning, and a belief that things will work out in the end, despite
unfavorable odds. This sense of meaning persists, even among children up-
rooted by wars or scattered as orphans and refugees to the four corners of the
earth. (p. 108)

Similarly, the role that story and personal narrative can play in establishing a continuity to an existence that regularly threatens discontinuity
should not be discounted. As was discussed in Chapter 4, the story mode
addresses the temporal basis of the child's search for meaning and purpose
in the world by linking past, present, and future into a single continuous
narrative. Garbarino and his associates (1992) echo a similar sentiment and
emphasize the potential buffering role that story can play in supporting
children in crisis:

'Stories,' such personal narratives, are an important resource in helping people
[to] cope with trauma and disaster. They give social meaning to personal
experience. They provide a basis for interpreting the present and acting on the
future. Such stories can be fundamental to the process of coping with adversity.
(p. 31)

Of course, children who are the victims of community violence cannot
be expected to cope solely on their own. They also require help from others,
particularly from caring adults who can provide them with consistently
high levels of support and security. It is perhaps not surprising, then, that
there is a significant correlation between resiliency in childhood and the
opportunity to establish a close bond with at least one adult who can
provide the child with continued stable care and attention, even despite the
crises unfolding around the child (Werner, 1990). This need seems to be
consistent regardless of the social context and is highlighted by a number of
writers whose research addresses the potentially pivotal role of the adult
caregiver in the lives of both the traumatized child *and the normal child*.
James Garbarino and his associates (1992) make this point particularly
clear:

As we steer away from single-issue, curricular interventions that focus on the
most negative aspects of these environments—gangs, sex, drugs, violence, and
so forth—toward more positive, educationally based, and individually focused
interventions, we emphasize the role of *caring relationships with significant*

adults as the principle agent of change and source of support. (p. 130, emphasis added)

Carol Gilligan (1985) generalizes this same need for adult support to all children:

> I think that one could assume that care is what children want. And in that sense, the wish for care and the belief that people should care and respond to one another is not a mother's perception, but rather a human perception that arises from the fact that no person—male or female—survives unless somebody, some adult, makes an attachment to that person.

In the spirit of the above quotations and the two quotations that open this chapter—one written within the context of the holistic tradition, the other from the perspective of the child as a victim of community violence—we might say that it is the adult's mediation of the child's experience of the world which is of central importance in helping children to deal effectively with the impact of community violence, but also with *the normal processes of growing up*.

Garbarino and his associates (1992) argue that what children need from adults are responses that are both "emotionally validating and developmentally challenging" (p. 11). Particularly during early and middle childhood, "the child's capacity to experience 'trust,'" they argue (p. 9), "depends on [their] ability to recognize continuity and regularity in care and caregivers." In the case of children living in the midst of social conflict, it is the adult's mediation of the violence that surrounds the child which helps the child to make sense of her world. These authors argue that adults need to be able to listen to children as they struggle to construct a narrative account of their lives. Adults need to be patient and compassionate as "children struggle to make sense of what fundamentally does *not* make sense" (p. 22).

In helping children to cope with the violence and uncertainty which surrounds them, adult caregivers can play three pivotal roles of support. As *supportive caregivers*, adults can provide at-risk children with consistently high levels of care, guardianship, and attention. In responding to the expressed need of children to find in adults, the sources of support required for healthy development into adulthood, adults can effectively serve as buffers of security and reassurance for children. As *enlightened witnesses* (A. Miller, 1990), caregivers can recognize and "make legitimate" the dangers facing children. They can help children to cope with the developmental and psychological consequences of social conflict. Finally, as *proactive advocates*, adults can, wherever possible, intervene on behalf of children.

They can attempt to mediate (or even permanently remove children from) the violent elements that permeate their lives. Furthermore, caregivers can help children to secure those social and community resources which can best help them to cope in the long term.

Parents, older siblings, and other family members are not the only adults children may turn to for support. Increasingly, teachers are also being called upon to play a more integral role in supporting children who are living in chronic danger. The influx of refugee children into the United States and Canada who are fleeing violence elsewhere in the world makes this a priority, but just as important, the school *as a refuge* for children presently living in danger in American and Canadian communities is increasingly becoming a recurrent theme in the lives of many students and teachers, especially those living and working in inner-city communities. In light of the importance attributed to the child's search for meaning and purpose in the world within the holistic philosophy, holistic educators, it is emphasized in this chapter, are uniquely positioned to respond effectively to the needs of such at-risk children as they struggle to establish a sense of security and find adult support in the precarious world of danger which permeates their lives. Indeed, the need to respond effectively to children living in danger also provides holistic educators with a unique opportunity to enter into the debate over the fundamental aims of schools. (However, if holistic educators are to offer constructive solutions to such challenges, they will also need to address the social justice issues inherent to the problem of community violence, which largely arise from the ethical realm of consciousness noted in Chapter 2.)

EARTH CRISIS AND THE GIFT OF TIME

An exploration of the impact of community violence on the lives of children provides a suitable (if tentative) context for understanding the destabilizing effects that dramatic environmental change may soon have on industrialized communities throughout the world. Environmental change is now already contributing to social conflict in the developing world. Homer-Dixon, Boutwell, and Rathjens (1993) have shown that in a number of developing countries, the depletion of resources, dramatic rises in the human population, and environmental pollution currently impact to varying degrees on the displacement of populations, increased regional and ethnic tensions, inequality of access to depleted resources, and a further weakening of the state structure. These researchers conclude that:

> Scarcities of renewable resources are already contributing to violent conflict in
> many parts of the developing world. These conflicts may foreshadow a surge

of similar violence in coming decades, particularly in poor countries where shortages of water, forests, and, especially, fertile land, coupled with rapidly expanding populations, already cause great hardship. (p. 38)

At present, industrialized nations would appear to be shielded from the most debilitating effects of dramatic environmental change. In part, this has been achieved by transferring such problems to developing countries (for example, by shipping harmful waste products to the developing world). But the industrialized world can hope to stave off the consequences of environmental degradation for only so long. Eventually, as the effects of the ecological crisis intensify, power imbalances between industrialized and developing nations will likely not be enough to protect even the world's richest citizens from the social conflicts now experienced by developing countries. [Even in industrialized countries at present, children are already among the first human victims of the ecological crisis, for they are more vulnerable to and affected by environmental pollution, including, in particular, cancer-causing agents and lead poisoning (Timberlake & Thomas, 1990).]

How do dire predictions for the future relate to the main argument of this book, namely, that the child's search for a functional cosmology of the universe during middle childhood presents us with a unique opportunity to change the course of human and earth history? Within the context of such an uncertain future, we might say that the success of such a proposal is dependent upon the child being purposefully granted a "gift of time" by adults—a protected period[2] of ten to twelve years (or more) following birth, in which she is able to become at home in the world, develop an ecologically sensitive relationship to the wider earth community, and build a functional cosmology of the universe. This chapter has argued that such a "gift" would need to be intrinsically related to the notion of childhood as a distinct ontological stage within the human life span and the need for adults to play a supportive, caregiving role in the lives of children. Only within such a design could the child begin to play an active role in the recovery of sustainable relations with the wider earth community.

CHAPTER 6

The Recovery of the Earth Process Through Childhood

For some two million years, we have had the capacity for language, storytell-ing, and ritual theater, launched by our older capacity for gesture and elabo-rated by our peculiar ability to use symbols for guiding us on our way through this world. During much of our history, animals have been among the key symbols we have used to sort out options for ourselves . . . And so, very early on in human evolution, we became naturalists.

—Gary Paul Nabhan and Stephen Trimble, *The Geography of Childhood: Why Children Need Wild Places* (1994)

In all cultures, the transmission of ideas and practices from generation to generation establishes the basis for survival and cultural life and ensures the continual renewal of the social fabric of society. Whether institutionally framed around schools and religious institutions or informally organized around families and clan groups on an apprenticeship-style basis, education has historically served as a primary vehicle for the transmission of cultural knowledge, practices, norms, values, attitudes, and skills to the next gener-ation. In any society, the foremost aim and obligation of education is to equip the youngest members of society with the cultural means for securing the future viability of that society. For most of recorded history, the aim of preserving those living traditions upon which cultural survival has de-pended has given education a *preservative* role in this regard. Cultures flourished by transferring from generation to generation the teachings of specific traditions and practices which stood the test of time and were fundamentally conserving in their treatment of the natural world. More recently in the modern era, this focus has been largely displaced by a *recon-structive* view of the educational process, comprising a successive series of intergenerational transformations in the physical and symbolic foundations of society. Driven by a futuristic vision of unlimited progress and technolog-

124

ical optimism, such a conception of education has made possible the striking changes and alterations to cultural (and now biological) life that we see at present.

One consequence of the reconstructive view of education is that we have largely lost the cultural sources of support that have sustained societies throughout history and rooted their cosmologies and patterns of social life within the context of nature's finite ability to support human life. (From this perspective, our current view of the educational process is actually regressive and dysfunctional.) Within traditional societies (e.g., Indigenous and Neolithic cultures), a biocentric world view and sustainable economic and technological practices underlay daily life, found cultural expression in the arts, and in human achievements. Oral culture and narrative provided the chief means by which ecologically sensitive values and norms were transmitted from elders to children. "Self" emerged as an extension of nature and "place." The cyclical quality of natural processes informed the underlying cosmology. This implicit vision of the human as a component member of a larger earth community, a vision so necessary for long-term cultural survival, is now largely lost to us in this modern, industrial era.

The need to recover a sense of connectedness to the natural world and to the wider earth community emerges as a primary cultural task if we are to respond effectively to the ecological challenge. Such a recovery will need to be multifaceted, involving persons of every age and profession, and all social institutions. This chapter explores some tentative proposals for the role that education and children might play within such a recovery. Although many aspects of the educational process deserve attention in this regard, the scope of this chapter is limited to the curricular and methodological foundations of an ecologically sensitive approach to education in middle childhood. Following from the basic position outlined in previous chapters, it is argued that the recovery of the ecological imperative in society should take account of the time-critical stage of middle childhood in which an ecologically sensitive cosmology can first take root and find expression in the child's search for a functional cosmology of the universe. It is within such a context that the following proposals arise.

A DEVELOPMENTALLY SENSITIVE CURRICULUM

It is the argument of this book that education during childhood should pay critical attention to children's inner motivations and time-critical stages of development in a way that marks a renewed alliance between curriculum and developmental psychology. Both the methodology and content of the curriculum should emerge from an analysis of how children perceive the world around them and interact with it on an ongoing basis. A primary observation (which we owe in large part to the architects of progressive education) is that children learn best through purposeful activity—when they play an active, participative role in their learning. The initiatives of progressive education are based largely on this first principle. A second observation is that for later learning to be successful, basic literacy and numeracy skills need to be reinforced in middle childhood, both on a direct instructional basis, but also as part of a larger, more inclusive language arts program. Basic literacy and numeracy skills are paramount within the design of an ecologically sensitive approach to education. (Indeed, they should be, as they provide the means for moving into new critical modes of relatedness to the world in adolescence.) These skills emerge both as part of an overall strategy for instruction in middle childhood, but also within the context of a holistic curriculum that provides numerous entry points for teaching and reinforcing basic skills by immersing children within a rich oral and written narrative classroom culture.

Jerome Harste and Kathy Short (1988) list a number of basic principles which they judge to be integral to the development of literacy in childhood. (Only a selected few are mentioned here.) First, learning should be functional. Children should feel that they are communicating for real purposes—to convey an idea, tell a story, relay a message, or argue a point. The notion that communication can serve multiple purposes needs to be encoded in the activities which lead to literacy from the very outset of the learning process. Second, the development of oral and written literacy is understood to be a social process, accomplished in large part through interaction with others. Teachers and peers fulfill an important role in this regard not only as the audience for a completed piece of writing, but also by providing editorial comments for writing-in-progress and by helping others to flesh out ideas for new writing projects. Third, the development of children's metacognitive thought processes (i.e., thinking about thinking) should be nurtured as children reflect on the meanings which they attribute to the phenomena they are writing about. Children need opportunities to reflect on their emerging understandings of the way the world works via the process of encoding such understandings in prose, drama, and art. Their written and artistic expression should provide them with the opportunity to communicate and organize their ideas and personal experiences in a way that reflects their developing understanding of the world. Finally, children's writing should be valued and celebrated as "the real thing" by providing children with opportunities to share their work with others and by using children's writing as the launching point for additional learning activities.

Although Harste and Short do not directly situate their proposals within the context of an ecologically sensitive curriculum, the principles they cite are conducive to the kinds of approaches to teaching and learning that we need to nurture in schools at present. Earlier chapters have represented middle childhood as the period during which children come to understand the world for themselves, to refine further their sense of self and build a functional cosmology of the universe. An elementary curriculum that helps children to co-construct with peers and adults alike a functional and ecologically sensitive view of the world can support the unfolding of this process and also prepare children for a more substantive and critical exploration of the ecological challenge in adolescence.

To support such efforts, learning in childhood now needs to be seen not simply as an intellectual exercise, well removed from the world outside the classroom, but rather as a cultural endeavor on the part of the child, who is building the foundations of an emerging cosmology of the world. In early childhood, "building things" largely meant framing an initial relationship to the world within the immediate environments of the child's life; but with the transition to middle childhood, such efforts now come to be directed toward the semantic and symbolic foundations of the wider culture and universe. The child's maturing conscious life propels her into a wider cultural field of thought than that afforded the younger child. The child's striving toward cultural self-fulfillment arises as a celebratory response to the child's emerging selfhood and newfound mastery over motion and mobility, language and thought. Much of the child's learning during this period is implicit, occurring not in the classroom, but on the playground, through exposure to television, and by way of the child's expanding social horizons—environments quite removed from the explicit teachings of the formal curriculum. The implicit lessons of childhood—the moral and social lessons of playground life, private moments of self-realization, shared experiences of achievement, chance encounters with others, and exposure to new environments—all have the potential to play deeply on the character of the child and in doing so reveal their essential power to shape children's basic orientations to the world. A curriculum that aims to nurture in children an ecologically sensitive view of the world needs to take heed of the fundamental qualities of these and other implicit experiences, to provide children with similarly compelling learning experiences that are richly rewarding, actively engaging, and conducive to the developmental tasks of middle childhood. While the proposals in this chapter highlight specific elements of an ecologically sensitive curriculum, it is emphasized that these ideas still need to be explicitly related to the milieu of particular classroom settings and local contexts and adapted to best meet the individual needs, interests, and dispositions of specific groups of children.

NATURAL MATERIALS IN THE CLASSROOM

In designing an ecologically sensitive curriculum, it is important to consider how the physical environment of the classroom can contribute to an overall strategy for learning. Partly in an effort to renew their ties to the natural world and counteract the industrial anomie of the world outside of school, children should be surrounded by objects, toys, and learning apparatus made from materials directly derived from nature and which nurture a sense of rootedness in the natural world.

In many ways, Waldorf school kindergartens epitomize the way in which natural materials could be incorporated into other levels of elementary education. Waldorf kindergartens favor nonfinished natural materials over manufactured toys whose functionality is limited by their intricate and specialized design. With nonfinished materials, children bring their own imaginations to the play materials, which, in turn, preserve for the child the natural integrity, texture, and imperfections of the original material. In Waldorf schools, writes Frans Carlgren (1976, p. 31), "a kindergarten contains as few finished things as possible . . . Above all there are stones, sea shells . . . twigs . . . clay objects, and decorative pieces of cloth . . . paper and wood."

Why do Waldorf schools explicitly incorporate natural elements into the physical design of the classroom? Waldorf educators believe that elemental materials such as wood, stone, clay, sand, and water have an eternal quality which transcends that of "man-made" substances and works on a subconscious level to reinforce subtly children's identification with nature. (Manufactured substances such as plastic do not share this same eternal quality, nor do they support children's identification with nature, but they do reflect the reality of human intervention in the natural world.) Having natural materials in the classroom does not simply fulfill children's aesthetic needs; rather, these materials also reach far back in time to embrace an age when the natural world provided the overriding context for all human activity, including recreation and learning:

> [A] lesson we have learned is the importance of imbuing physical settings for children with the sense of being in nature. Natural things have three qualities that are unique: their unending diversity, the fact that they are not created by people, and their feeling of timelessness—the mountain, river, or trees described in fairy tales and myths still exist today. These qualities would seem to show children a different reality from that of man-made articles. (Prescott, 1987, p. 87)

Surrounding children with natural materials within the confines of the classroom represents a laudable first step, but children also need to be given opportunities to interact with these materials in meaningful ways—for example, through their play activity in early childhood and by way of handicrafts such as woodworking, stone masonry, and pottery in middle childhood and adolescence. Nor should the historical significance of such artisan activities to previous generations be lost on children. Within a holistic curriculum, the teaching of handicrafts can build connections between the subject areas of fine art, history, and natural history, foster children's creative expression, and help them to develop skills related to fine motor and hand–eye coordination.

THE SPIRIT OF PLACE

Methodological and curricular reforms inside the school and classroom are integral to an ecologically sensitive approach to education, but the school is only one of several institutions and social conditions which touch the lives of children. In Chapter 3, a cosmological model of childhood was presented which highlighted a number of important factors that influence the social conditions of childhood. A complementary model that situates human development within an ecological view of the web of interactions between child and community is forwarded by Urie Bronfenbrenner (1979). Bronfenbrenner argues that learning and development proceed in a dynamic way as the result of interactions between children and the various environmental systems that mediate their lives. Some systems, such as the family or peer group, directly impact on the lives of children, while others, such the local planning authority and legal institutions, have a more indirect, but no less pervasive, influence.

Within an ecological model of place (see Figure 6.1), the local community — whether it be a metropolitan city, a small town, a village, or a farming community — is viewed as an ecosystem with feedback connections that integrate the infrastructure of the community and its institutions, market economies, cultural groups, and other features with the natural and built environments that define the community's living space. Learning how communities function as ecosystems can help children to appreciate more fully the biological and cultural interdependencies which sustain their living space *and the living space of other species*. To know one's place is to have an intimate knowledge of the local environment (both natural and built) and the various professional roles, shared histories, and interdependent relationships that sustain the community over the long term. To further strengthen children's ties to the local community, their participation in community projects that help to nurture culturally significant relationships between young and old can be fostered by way of apprenticeship-style programs and community renewal efforts that arise within ecologically sustainable contexts.

Figure 6.1 The Ecology of Place in Childhood

The Saginaw River Project in Saginaw, Michigan (Pelkki, 1994) is a good example of a school/community initiative with ecological roots. Responding to health concerns regarding the water quality of the Saginaw River, elementary and secondary school students in 1989 began conducting regular water quality tests of the Saginaw River. Their results showed an alarmingly high fecal coliform count that soon led public health officials to institute new safety measures for use of the river. Had the Saginaw project ended here, it would have already made an important contribution in improving the public health of the local community. However, as the project moved forward, teachers began to find new learning possibilities that emerged out of a broader view of the cultural and ecological interdependencies that connected the river to the local community. Jo Ann Pelkki reflects on teachers' dawning awareness of the educational potential of a more comprehensive river study:

> As the project to test the river progressed, the teachers . . . began to see the River Project in different ways. Why not look at the river not only as a geographic entity, but also as a factor in the history, politics, culture, commerce, and recreation of our city? . . . [Soon] students were busy researching other aspects of the river, and writing, drawing, photographing, and talking about it . . . Some students went to the library to read about the history of the city and how the river affected the development of our community. They talked to local historians and history buffs and went on to write stories, poems, and other accounts relating to the river . . . Students in a Media Broadcasting class were given the opportunity to make a documentary about all of the activities going on in our schools, relating to the river. (p. 32)

This project originally began as a simple water quality initiative but soon blossomed into a interdisciplinary project that connected the diverse subject areas of ecology, natural history, environmental activism, and media literacy. Among the outcomes of the Saginaw River Project are a series of poetry books, a one-hour video documentary, and regular "rivercasts" that report biweekly on the continuing successes of the project.

Nonecological approaches to the study of the place are already evident in many elementary schools today. Through the study of the local community, data gathering, interviewing, and other research skills are learned and applied. Folk tales and historic records of the local community are compiled. Paintings by local artists, old photographs, monuments, and other media are analyzed for common or divergent threads of meaning. In ethnically diverse communities, the multicultural experience of place is deepened through visits to settings that incorporate a variety of architectural styles and cultural icons. But such efforts now need to be complemented by activities that actively promote an ecological awareness in children. The environmental health of the local community and the characteristics of the wider bioregion need to become important frames of reference in planning for the study of place in middle childhood. Visits to the school by adult role models who perform key roles in sustaining the ecological and cultural infrastructure of the community need to become more commonplace. The study of the flow of energy and waste products through the local community needs to be seen as an appropriate forum for introducing early adolescents to the basic principles of environmental and community economics.

In the upper elementary and secondary grades, a series of key questions can be posed to students in an effort to help them focus on specific ecological and community concerns. Students can be asked to consider the following: What is the relationship between the built and natural environments of the local community? How have local residents used the natural surroundings to enhance the aesthetic value of the community as a whole? Through its various stages of development, has the built environment come to dominate its natural surroundings, or has the community intentionally preserved open spaces, vegetation, water bodies, and other natural features of the local bioregion? At a cultural level, how are public and private spaces defined? Are there specific features of the local community that act as meeting places to foster community life? What efforts are being made to preserve or restore old and historic buildings, and is the preservation of local heritage (both natural and built) viewed as a priority by local residents? These and other questions can help teachers frame the study of place within a context that promotes ecological and community renewal.

As a philosophical undertaking, the study of place is not only relevant to education in middle childhood, but also to an ecologically sensitive approach to education in adolescence, particularly as students begin to wrestle with the impact of rapid technological change on society. Contemporary notions of place which for centuries have been grounded in the physical experience of neighborhoods and local communities now face serious challenges as networks of individuals linked by global telecommunications replace face-to-face meetings between people and as "virtual places" in the digital world of web sites and the Internet replace firsthand contact with people and places in the real world of local communities. The lasting impact of such a fundamental shift in our lifestyles and notions of "community" and "self" are yet to be worked out. However, it seems clear that such a fundamental reworking of place will continue to have far-reaching consequences within most industrialized societies. Viewed within this context, the study of place in middle childhood can serve as a valuable launching point for exploring the sociocultural and psychological implications of rapid technological innovation to changing notions of social and community life.

Although the study of place can represent an engaging line of inquiry in both middle childhood and adolescence, it also raises important concerns related to the quality of children's environments in many communities around the world. In light of the focus of the previous chapter and considering the scale of community violence and environmental degradation that afflicts many communities in the United States, Canada, and elsewhere at present, serious questions can be raised about the feasibility — and desirability — of involving students in a study of their local communities in middle childhood. To be effective, the study of place clearly requires that neighborhoods afford to children and other residents a sense of security in their daily lives. When such security cannot be assured, it falls to adults to take the necessary action that will restore appropriate levels of community support for children. The absence of the study of place in schools due to concerns about the quality of the local community does not relieve adults from their responsibility to make communities safe for children. On the contrary, such concerns should alert caregivers and other citizens of the urgent need for action to improve the safety and quality of the local community for children and adults alike.

One encouraging sign of ecological and community renewal at present is the growing number of school/community partnerships around the world which aim to bring nature back into the city by restoring selected areas of school grounds to their natural states (see Table 6.1). In recent years, students, teachers, parents, local businesses, and community residents have worked together in city centers across the United States, Canada, Great Britain, and elsewhere to turn concrete playgrounds into vegetable and herb gardens, bird and butterfly habitats, prairie gardens, and woodland forests. School ground naturalization projects provide naturalized play and learning spaces for children, serve as immediately accessible field study centers for hands-on environmental education activities, and enhance the aesthetics of the local neighborhood (Evergreen Foundation, 1994). In many cases, students and teachers have researched the natural history of a site and the

Table 6.1. Ecologically Sensitive Education in Urban Settings

A Toronto school has adopted an innovative approach to ecologically sensitive reform. In an ongoing effort to bring nature "to the doorstep" of children living in the city, a local elementary school has turned parts of the school's concrete playground into a wilderness garden:

With a series of private, corporate and foundation donations, school fundraising projects, government grants and a lot of volunteer blood, sweat and tears, the greening of the Ossington–Old Orchard school yard has [begun]....There's an upland forest and a vegetable garden. They've put in an apple orchard and now they're talking about an irrigation system that would operate all summer on a timer. Even the baseball diamond was grassed over: the kids still play baseball there, but they're running around on grass and earth instead of concrete and asphalt. There's an aviary designed to attract birds and butterflies; an area of wildflower meadows; and a variety of 45 native plant species thriving in the wooded areas. (Dineen, 1992)

The reform efforts initiated by parents, teachers, and local residents over the past several years in this school community have had a direct impact on the curriculum of the school and served as an effective model for several initiatives elsewhere in the city. Children and teachers garden, grow their own food, host a harvest festival each autumn, and learn about nature and ecology through direct contact with the natural world surrounding the school. Plans are currently in the works for a tree house classroom and amphitheater design competition.

wider bioregion as part of the planning process to make certain that only those plant species which are well suited to local soil and climate conditions are reintroduced. School ground naturalization projects require a long-term commitment from a core group of supporters, a well-organized planning process, and a sustained vision that attracts community support, but once under way, these projects offer a rich variety of curricular possibilities for hands-on environmental education and nature study. By creatively integrating these naturalized environments into the everyday curriculum, teachers can ensure that these initiatives are valued and sustained over the long term.

GARDENING

Ask city children today where the food they eat originally came from and many will likely have a difficult time tracing the food chain back farther than the local supermarket. This inability to relate the nourishment one receives to the sustenance provided by the wider earth community is symptomatic of a culture that has largely lost touch with its dependence on the natural world. In an effort to counteract such a loss, gardening in schools can emerge as a central activity in early and middle childhood (where seasonally feasible) and offer both children and teachers a refreshing and participative approach to nature education:

> Our children need to learn gardening. The reasons for this reach deep into their mental and emotional, as well as into their physical survival. Gardening is an active participation in the deepest mysteries of the universe. By gardening, our children learn that they constitute, with all growing things, a single community of life. They learn to nurture and be nurtured in a universe that is always precarious, but ultimately benign. They learn profound reasons for the seasonal rituals of the great religious traditions . . . Elementary education especially might very well begin and be developed in a gardening context. (Berry, 1989, p. 3)

Tending a garden reinforces basic values related to responsibility and care, but such an exercise also actively involves children in a ongoing study of the cyclical processes of growth, decay, and the rebirth of life. As gardeners, children have a stake in the outcome of their work, and this in turn helps them to develop a deeper appreciation for the sustenance requirements of living things. On a firsthand basis, children learn about the need for plants to receive adequate amounts of sunlight, water, and nutrients, and they begin to recognize the importance of their own role in cultivating these plants over the long term. When such projects are carried on over a period of successive years, a genuine link is forged between children's gardening endeavors and the moral/character goals of instilling ecologically sensitive values and skills related to children's interaction with nature.

Although it is an important learning activity unto itself, gardening can also serve to extend the study of place and the local community in schools. In the Common Roots program, a Vermont-based eco-literacy initiative (Food Works, 1992), elementary school children grow "historical theme gardens" and learn about the various cultural and historical practices that connect the themes of food, community, and ecology. The Common Roots program goes far beyond a traditional gardening strategy by contextualizing children's gardening endeavors within the study of the local bioregion, folklore, and historical and sustainable approaches to gardening. By focusing on food as a cultural and ecological system of exchanges, children in this program learn about the connections that can be made between the ecological practice of gardening and the cultural/historical practices of growing, preparing, and sharing food.

Even the most concrete-laden school environment likely hides small patches of topsoil that can serve as starting points for children's gardening projects. These areas may be out of the way and overlooked by most children and adults in their daily activities, but for the astute and observant teacher they can nevertheless serve as the impetus for gardening projects that actively engage students in a study of nature. As a culminating activity at the end of the gardening season, children can invite parents and other visitors to a harvest festival, complete with garden salads and other delicacies grown and prepared by the children that celebrate their achievements in gardening and the nourishment provided by the natural environment surrounding the school.

THE STUDY OF FORM

Gardening has served as a life-sustaining activity for humans ever since the beginning of the agricultural revolution some 35,000 years ago. The ever-renewing seasonal cycles of nature have contextualized the ways in which we have made sense of the world, by framing our notions of time, place, and nature, etc. But making sense of the world has also been highlighted in this and previous chapters as a primary cultural task of middle childhood. With reference to Rudolf Steiner, it has been argued that the rhythmic processes of middle childhood are at the very heart of the child's search for meaningfulness, purpose, reciprocity, and continuity in the world. Perhaps no set of learning activities better addresses this search than the study of rhythm and form in nature, art, architecture, mathematics, music, and other cultural pursuits. When children are invited to search for the essential patterns, rhythms, and divergences which give both nature and art their aesthetic appeal, the child's search for meaningfulness and purpose in the world is likely to emerge within an ecologically sensitive context that is congruent with nature's own strategies for preserving the integral dimensions of the earth process. As Marcus Schneck (1991) writes:

> Once nature finds something that works, be it pattern, color, shape, or form, that special something is repeated again and again. . . . Patterns in nature are the keys that help us learn about, remember, and link elements of the world around us. Once we've assimilated knowledge about a particular pattern, we can extend that knowledge to new and unfamiliar situations where that same pattern occurs. (pp. 11, 13)

Peter S. Stevens (1974) expresses a similar sentiment:

> Our subject concerns the visual patterns and forms in the natural world. It turns out that those patterns and forms are peculiarly restricted, that the immense variety that nature creates emerges from the working and reworking of only a few formal themes. . . . The rules are rigorous, but within those rules variety abounds, and the rules show through the variations to portray a relatedness of parts that is aesthetically pleasing and a constancy of purpose that provides an eternal model for all of man's creations. (pp. 3, 222)

The study of form—the search for patterns of integration and differentiation in the natural, physical, and cultural worlds that surround the child—is integral to an ecologically sensitive approach to education during middle childhood. Children can study spiraling, meandering, and branching patterns in nature and compare these patterns to their human equivalents in the cultural world of art and music. An analysis of the scales of pineapples and pine cones can help children in the advanced grades to uncover the Fibonacci numbers and lead to the discovery of other mathematical principles of natural form. Children can structure their study of form by size and search for repeating patterns on a variety of scales from the vast to the microscopic. The study of elemental colors and shapes, including spheres, hexagons, and stripes, can lead into an investigation of the camouflage strategies employed by a variety of species. In the upper elementary grades, rudimentary mathematical equations and geometric forms that map natural occurrences can be introduced, as can computer models that represent complex systems and natural fractals. The study of patterns in nature can serve as a foray into a more advanced investigation of complex systems and the tenets of chaos theory. In these and many other ways the study of form can serve as an interdisciplinary exploration that integrates the aesthetic appreciation of nature and culture with a general introduction to many of the physical properties of the universe as a whole:

> Whenever we look in the world we find geometrical forms: the pattern of a snowflake, the hexagonal honeycomb, the many-sided crystal, the parabola of a trajectory, the spiral of a snail's shell, the regular pattern of leaves on many plants, the proportions of the golden mean as applied to the human body. . . . and there have been artists who have surpassed all others in discovering the secrets of geometric relationships, weaving them into their paintings like an invisible skeleton, an imperceptible pattern which gives their work a stamp of supreme harmony. . . . To discover the geometric laws in the universe and in art can be a deeply joyful experience. The two different languages of art and science can merge into one at such moments. (Carlgren, 1976, p. 42)

From the above examples, it is clear that the study of form presents teachers with a wide array of curricular possibilities that can support children's search for meaningfulness and purpose in the world. However, such a curriculum needs to be well planned and grounded if it is to nurture effectively an ecologically sensitive view of the world. One way of framing the study of form is through the implicit use of guiding metaphors which tailor learning activities to achieve specific outcomes. By helping children to see the world from a specific vantage point—for example, as the working and reworking of a few formal themes—the curriculum can foster in children an ecologically sensitive vision of human continuity with the natural world.

One important guiding metaphor is the principle of the curvature of space. This principle has been used primarily by quantum physicists and cosmologists to characterize the continually creative yet order-giving character of the universe as an ongoing and ever-emergent process. Essentially, this principle aims to explain patterns of integration (common forms and origins) and instances of differentiation (uniqueness and subjectivity) which exist throughout the world. It seeks to account for such disparate phenomena as the similar branching patterns of rivers, trees, and arteries and the intricate patterns of snowflakes, each unique unto itself but collectively exhibiting a common form. As Brian Swimme and Thomas Berry (1992) note, the curvature of space

> is bound up with the energy of the universe's primordial Flaring Forth. Had the curvature been a fraction larger, the universe would have immediately collapsed down into a massive black hole; had it been a fraction smaller the universe would have exploded into a scattering of lifeless particles. . . . The expansive original energy keeps the universe from collapsing, while the gravitational attraction holds the component parts together and enables the universe

to blossom. Thus the curvature of the universe is sufficiently closed to maintain a coherence of its various components and sufficiently open to allow for a continued creativity. (p. 260)

One can picture the metaphor of the curvature of space as a semi-enclosed arc. The arc must be closed enough to articulate repeated recognizable forms and sustained patterns, but open enough to allow a diversity of forms and patterns to emerge. Hence the universe performs something of a balancing act in preserving the essential cohesion of sustained patterns and forms, while simultaneously allowing a diversity of variations on these forms and patterns to be articulated. As one of the most important ordering principles of the universe, the curvature of space principle establishes the cosmos as an order-creating, patterned universe that celebrates diversity within the context of structured form. Likeness but difference, integration but differentiation—this is the basic rule that preserves nature's integrity while ensuring that the creative evolutionary process continues to unfold.[1]

In many respects, nonecological lessons that reinforce an understanding of the curvature of space principle are already evident in schools today. Multicultural activities help children to appreciate and celebrate cultural differences (differentiation) while reminding children that people of different cultural backgrounds also share many things in common (integration). Team sports encourage children to excel as individuals (differentiation) within the context of learning to be team players (integration). Less formally, playground politics pit the ambitions of the individual child against the social pressures of the peer group. These and other examples demonstrate that there are clear moral and social lessons that can be drawn from an appreciation of the processes of integration and differentiation, particularly when these processes are applied to concrete situations that children can identify with easily.

Although the curvature of space principle and other metaphors can be explicitly introduced to older children and adolescents as helpful vantage points from which to perceive the world, it does not follow that such metaphors should be taught to younger children on a verbatim basis, as presented above. Rather, the types of learning activities in which children participate during middle childhood should gradually lead them to discern these principles for themselves. Through the close observation of nature, form drawing, studies of local geography, mathematical investigations, and the like, children should gradually come to see that the integral processes of integration and differentiation are continuously at work throughout the world, reflected both in the forms and functions of nature and in the artistic and cultural achievements of humans. Through the study of form, the child strengthens her powers of observation (of nature's patterns, rhythms, and symmetries), enhances her appreciation of the uniqueness of living things (everything has its own voice), and builds the basis of an ecologically sensitive cosmology that celebrates human continuity with the natural world.

THE STORY OF THE UNIVERSE

An ecologically sensitive approach to education incorporates not only a spatial view of the universe rooted within the study of place and nature, but also a temporal vision of the unfolding of the universe through time. Such an approach roughly corresponds to the traditional place accorded history in schools, save for two important exceptions. First, an ecologically sensitive approach to history counters the typically anthropocentric nature of the traditional history program by situating history within a "natural history" context. Second, by paying critical attention to how children relate to the world during middle childhood, an earth-centered approach to history emerges within a narrative context that engages the child's imagination.

In the modern era, the teaching of history has typically been limited to the study of the human world with little or no regard for the integration of the wider ecological patterns upon which the human world has depended. More often than not, the nonhuman world has been viewed as no more than a distant backdrop upon which the more important drama of human history has unfolded. This omission has been exasperated by the fact that human history has generally been framed as a progressive endeavor—a progression *into* the foreground and *away from* an interdependency with the natural world—even as the human relationship to nature has gradually deteriorated to the point where our actions at present threaten the future viability of the natural world. As C. A. Bowers (1993) notes:

> Presentations of history involve putting humans in the foreground—their thoughts, artistic achievements, wars, political struggles, technological developments, and so on. This anthropocentric bias is further strengthened by representing social change as the expression of progress. This narrative tradition seldom gives an adequate account of how different aspects of cultural development—political and religious ideas, arts, technologies, and economic practices, etc.—were influenced by the unique features of the local ecosystems. Nor does it provide an adequate understanding of the culture's impact on soil fertility, wildlife, and the nonrenewable elements of the environment. Historical understanding should situate humans in the context of natural systems, and it should avoid anesthetizing students with the myth of progress. (p. 170)

By reframing history within a biocentric context, by giving voice to the integration of human history with the changing patterns of the natural world, an ecologically sensitive approach to education counters the implicit anthropocentricism which pervades most history teaching and points to new pathways for exploration. Some of the themes which emerge within a biocentric view of history include: how human settlement patterns and agricultural practices have been shaped over time by conditions in the natural world; how wars and other conflicts have been prompted by competition over scarce (or plentiful) resources; how the natural world has informed the underlying cosmologies of aboriginal communities and early Neolithic civilizations; and the history of ecologically sustainable technological, economic, and social practices.

On one hand, framing history within a natural history context serves as an important corrective measure insofar as it challenges the anthropocentric foundations of contemporary approaches to history teaching, but such a reorientation can also have a deeper significance. It can ground our understanding of the world within those points of origin which we all have in common and which we share collectively with other species. It can challenge those ahistorical tendencies within modern technological society which not so subtly dismiss the relevance of the past to the promise of some new future technological age. Cultivating a sense of historicity within a biocentric context emerges as a fundamental goal of an ecologically sensitive approach to education and underscores the historic commitments of humans both to each other and to the natural world:

> A sense of history reminds us of our commitments as well as the ways in which we have responded to them. It also urges us to be connected with [that which] we will never personally know, [those] who lived before us and those not yet born. We are all connected by history and our sense of harmony derives from a sense of a common history of struggle. History is the repository of the human struggle for meaning and represents the connection between memory and response. . . . The responsibility for humanity to participate in its destiny [and the destiny of the wider earth community] is central to a conception of an education directed toward a loving, compassionate, and just world. (Purpel, 1989, p. 127)

By going one step further, by offering children and adolescents something more than a simple reformulation of recent political or national history—perhaps by taking a cue from Maria Montessori and offering children the story of the universe—we build on the child's inherent sense of wonder and her capacity to enter into the unfolding earth process in an imaginative and engaging way. The story of the universe entails both the history of the earth community before humans "made their mark" on the planet (including the successive series of geological and biological changes leading up to the emergence of the human) and also a more integral understanding of how the wider earth community has served to contextualize human activity throughout the modern period. A recent effort by cosmologist Brian

Swimme and cultural historian Thomas Berry (1992) to present a comprehensive, if formative, narrative account of the universe story is sketched in the paragraphs below—from the primordial "flaring forth" to the rise of the first human communities—and reveals a plethora of curricular possibilities for an ecologically sensitive approach to education:

Fifteen billion years ago, in a momentous burst of energy never to be equaled again, the universe was formed in a great flash which sent gaseous matter spewing out in all directions. Over a billion years passed before this great energy burst was calm and stable enough to organize the gaseous matter into the over one hundred billion galaxies which comprise the universe as we know it today. These galaxies functioned as giant self-organizing systems of energy, hurtling through empty space for the next several billion years. These were turbulent years. The most luminous stars matured quickly and exploded into powerful supernovas that marked the birth of new systems of energy. These second generation systems were more promising in their potentiality, more elaborate in their internal structure, and held the essential elements of life: carbon, nitrogen, oxygen, and the other elements. Ten billion years after the initial burst of energy, our Milky Way galaxy formed as a second generation system and with it ten thousand new stars. One of the these stars was the Sun. In a massive burst of energy, the Sun blasted off all of the gaseous matter which encircled it. Out of this energy burst was spun the solar system of Sun, Mercury, Venus, Earth, Mars, Jupiter, Saturn, Uranus, Neptune, and Pluto.

Not all of the planets in our solar system were bestowed with the same creative life potential as Earth. On Jupiter, Saturn, Neptune, and Uranus, the molten and gaseous activity never matured beyond the simplest chemical processes. On Mercury, Venus, Mars, and Pluto, the planetary crust slowly hardened into lifeless continents. Only the Earth, perfectly balanced as it was in its own internal dynamics and place within the solar system, displayed the creative chemical activity which was necessary for life to evolve.

The first cells to appear harnessed and channeled the life-giving powers of the original energy burst and coupled these powers with a newfound ability to remember the specific patterns of genetic information necessary for self-reproduction. The next incarnation of cells not only retained these abilities, but also harnessed the life-giving powers of oxygen. Meiotic sex, the union of two genetically unique organisms for the purpose of creating a third, also emerged at this time and increased the genetic variety of life multifold. On a complementary basis, predator/prey relations began to develop, and, coupled with the intimacy of meiotic sex, underscored both the symbiotic and violent dimensions of the emergent earth process. The culmination of all this creative activity was signaled by the development of the first multi-celled organism some seven hundred million years ago.

The emergence of the first multi-celled organisms set the stage for the propagation of a diversity of forms in nature. Corals, worms, insects, clams, jellyfish, starfish, sponges, spiders, vertebrates, leeches, and other species began to flourish. Gradually, species adapted themselves to meet the challenges of nature and the adaptations of other species. Snails developed shell casings to better protect themselves. New forms of locomotion emerged. Winged insects learned to propel themselves through the water. Fish developed bony fins to also move faster. Ocean tides cast plant life onto the land. Animal life soon followed, and so gradually emerged the great reign of amphibious creatures, and in time, the dinosaurs.

The creative dimensions of this early formative period did not go unchallenged. Disasters occasionally befell the earth, as massive astronomical collisions disrupted the delicate functioning of the earth's underlying processes. At times, life virtually had to reinvent itself, as with the extinction of the dinosaurs some 67,000,000 years ago. Yet this destruction also heralded the possibility of there arising new evolutionary lines of development. With the extinction of the dinosaurs, the integral creative dimensions of the earth process were sustained as mammals, birds, and other creatures rose to take their place in the great drama of life. With the development of mammalian life there also arose the capacity for emotional sensitivity via an increasingly complex nervous system and gradually, with the emergence of the human, conscious self-awareness.

Four million years ago in Africa humans first stood erect. Two million years ago humans learned to fashion simple tools. One and a half million years ago humans harnessed the power of fire. Thirty-five thousand years ago, humans first celebrated their emerging self-awareness through the ritualistic performances of festivals, ceremonies, and cave paintings. The domestication of plants and animals soon followed and signaled the gradual decline of hunter–gatherer societies and the emergence of small Neolithic villages and other settlements. New forms of cultural activity flourished in these settlements. Women held coveted roles in providing moral and religious leadership. Artists and artisans worked their crafts. Spiritual disciplines celebrated and articulated the celestial rhythms of nature and paid tribute to the divine Spirit. Many of the basic symbolic foundations of language emerged at this time. Developments in language, the arts, religion, and cosmology established the formative practices that even today comprise the basis of many artistic, spiritual, and symbolic disciplines.

In the above discussion, the universe story is retold by Brian Swimme and Thomas Berry largely from a Western scientific and historical point of view. (This story is taken up again later in this chapter, beginning with the emergence of the classical civilizations.) However, as these authors are quick to acknowledge, there are equally compelling interpretations of the universe story to be found within any number of cultural and religious traditions (e.g., Caduto and Bruchac, 1989). Throughout history the story of the universe has been told in many different ways and by various peoples around the world—from the earliest cosmologies of ancient civilizations to the scientific discoveries of the present age. The criterion for valuing a universe story does not rest solely in the story's "rightness" or "wrongness" as judged from a Western scientific vantage point, for example, but in the degree to which it offers a community a functional and ecologically sustainable vision of the human in relationship to other humans and the wider earth community.

A timeline can be used to introduce children to the story of the universe and is particularly effective in framing the immense scale of geological time which passed long before the human species came on the scene. Children can be asked to build a personal time-line, to trace their own individual history by recording those life events which are most important them. This personal time-line can then be used as the basis for introducing narratives and other learning activities which use writing, art, dance, drama, and music to explore the common histories of peoples and other species: familial history, cultural history, national history, world history, and earth history:

> In order to fully understand the story of the universe, the child needs a time connection. We begin with one of the happiest times of a child's life—his birthday. He makes a simple graph. Then the timeline of his life is compared to those of his family. His family lifeline is grafted onto the history timeline of man. . . . Units are no longer birthdays, but centuries. Finally, human time is projected onto geological eras—Paleozoic, Mesozoic, etc. (Kahn, 1980, p. 13)

In Montessori schools, the story of the universe is told to children over a period of weeks, months, or even years. Similarly, Waldorf schools organize the curriculum of the elementary years around specific epochs in human and earth history. Although the use of maps, charts, and pictures can help to extend and concretize the story of the universe, this story is often best told from memory, without the use of pictures or props, and in an engaging way that evokes each child's imagination. A curriculum that immerses children within the universe story can naturally lead to the study of a variety of subjects, including physical geography, weather, the seasons, taxonomy, and mineralogy.

A narrative approach to teaching and learning marks the return of a traditional strategy for transmitting ecological and cultural understandings to children. Within many societies and religious traditions, including Aboriginal and Eastern cultures, the narrative mode has historically served as a primary vehicle for transmitting cultural knowledge and practices to the youngest generation. Within such societies, cultural survival has depended in large part on the gradual induction of children into the implicit wisdom of deeply held cultural stories, myths, and other narratives. Encoded within such stories are the guiding metaphors and moral codes which frame not only the social organization of the culture, but also its relationship to the wider earth community and the even wider numinous universe comprising human, nature, and spirit.

What Western societies are now only beginning to rediscover, Indigenous, Eastern, and Neolithic cultures recognized and practiced long ago. The narrative mode establishes a sense of continuity to existence, addresses the temporal basis of the child's search for meaningfulness and purpose in the world, and sustains culturally significant relationships between young and old. Traditional systems of education are based on an intuitive understanding of the developmental processes of middle childhood, for it is during this period that the authority of stories (and the real and mythic adventures of heroes and otherworldly tales) gains such favor with children. Through story, time is given continuity and patterned form. And through metaphor, analogy, identification with heroes, moral parables, and the like, the richness and subtlety of a worldly cosmology is transmitted from one generation to the next.

With its own tales of grandeur and adventure, the story of the universe emerges as a logical extension to the child's search for a personal history. When told from a narrative point of view and in a participatory manner that evokes the creative intelligence of the child, this story not only has the potential to engage the child's imagination; it may also satisfy a need within the child to discover his own personal growth and development to be an extension of the universe story. During the most magical and eloquent of moments, perhaps during a period of intense creative activity or a quiet moment of reflection, the stories of self and universe may be intricately bound together in a single continuous drama that embraces the common origins of each.

EARTH LITERACY: THE CONCEPTS

At a cognitive level, educators need to challenge the basic assumptions and guiding metaphors which have underlaid and legitimated the human treatment of the natural world during the modern era. These assumptions are mythic in origin and have been fuelled by a dysfunctional vision of nature as an infinite resource, the myth of unending progress, overconsumption in industrialized nations, and the estrangement of the human from the natural world. Such guiding metaphors cannot be effectively countered solely by making children (and adults) aware of the flaws of this industrial world view; rather, a new set of implicit assumptions and guiding metaphors that arise from an ecological and biological understanding of how life functions also need to be introduced. Such understandings point to the dependency of the human on the natural world and provide the basis for an incisive critique of the industrial worldview beginning at or just prior to adolescence, as the child's critical faculties mature. It is suggested that four basic ecological understandings could provide the foundations for ecological literacy in middle childhood. These understandings are originally forwarded by Steve Van Matre in *Earth Education: A New Beginning* (1990).

The Flow of Energy. Sunlight is the prime mover in the great chemical cycles that provide the principle forms of energy for the earth and its inhabitants. The process of *photosynthesis* is the means by which sunlight is captured by green plants, which turn the sun's energy into starch-based molecules for consumption by other living organisms (through digestion). Within this process, energy flows through a *food chain*, from the sun to *producers* (green plants), to *herbivores* (plant-eating animals), and to *carnivores* (meat-eating animals). (*Decomposers* such as bacteria, fungi, and other microorganisms also play a critical role in this process as they break down and consume energy from the excrement and dead bodies of plants and animals.) As energy moves through the system and to higher levels of the food chain, much of it is naturally dissipated through the inefficiency of the energy transfer or used up as a result of the energy requirements of organisms (e.g., for mobility, growth, and tissue repair). The gradual dissipation (and degradation) of energy means that those at higher levels of the food chain, such as carnivores, need to consume significantly more energy than do those at lower levels of the food chain in order to meet their respective energy requirements. Hence the food chain can be seen as a pyramid where a broad base of green plants support increasingly fewer animals as energy flows upward through the system.

The Cycling of Matter. The biosphere comprises the topmost layer of the earth's surface—soil, water, gaseous atmosphere, minerals, nutrients, and organisms. Complex and fragile balances exist between the basic building materials of the biosphere—hydrogen, carbon, oxygen, nitrogen, phosphorous, sulfur, and other elements. These elements have been used and reused for millions of years by organisms that have "borrowed" and then "returned" them to the soil, water, and atmosphere in a continuous and unending cycle. The *soil cycle* comprises the movement of these elements through the food chain and back into the soil, where the decay of excrement and dead animals and plants releases rich nutrients back into the system. The *water cycle* comprises the evaporation of water from lakes, rivers, and oceans into the atmosphere, where it is condensed into clouds. When the clouds become too top heavy, water is released in the form of precipitation. Rain and snow fall to earth, some of it absorbed by plant and animal organisms. Water eventually flows back to lakes, rivers, and oceans to begin the cycle anew. The *air cycle* comprises the exchange of oxygen and carbon dioxide gases between animals and plants and also the release and movement of other particles into the atmosphere.

The Interrelating of Life. All life is integrally connected with all other aspects of life, and no organism can survive in isolation from the elements of life upon which it is dependent. It is the diversity of species within communities which allows life to thrive. Within communities, individual species fulfill complementary roles—their *niches*—by releasing rich nutrients into the soil or by controlling the population of another species, for example. In the natural world, a *community* comprises the diversity of plant, animal, and other species that are able to meet their basic survival needs within the context of the energy and material resources provided by a given space. Complex physical, chemical, and ecological relationships and interdependencies bind communities of animal and plant species together within their nonliving *habitats* (i.e., living spaces) to form *ecosystems*.

The Changing of Forms. Although the above understandings point to an inherent regenerative attitude in nature, the natural world also reveals an inexorable drive toward experimentation and adaptation as new species replace old and as organisms adapt to changing environmental conditions. *Evolution* comprises changes to the genetic makeup of species, perhaps over a few generations or over millions of years, as organisms improve in their ability to meet the demands of local conditions. The temporal basis of life is reflected in other ways as well. Some microorganisms have a life span of only a few days or even hours. In sharp contrast, the growth and movement of continents, mountains, and glaciers (i.e., geological time) takes many thousands of years.

The above understandings describe specific ecological processes, but just as important, they serve as metaphors for the interdependency of life on earth and the rhythmic (i.e., cyclical) nature of ecological systems. During middle childhood, the metaphorical wisdom inherent in such understandings is just as important as the explicit details these understandings reveal. When these processes are creatively introduced to the child in a concrete way, the child's developing cosmology of the universe is subtly reinforced by such understandings, not only on a cognitive level, but also at the level of imagination, as she attends to the metaphorical significance of such an ecological vision of the world.

EDUCATION IN ADOLESCENCE

If we were to trace the path of an ecologically sensitive approach to education beyond middle childhood and into adolescence, then it would be at or just prior to adolescence that the child's education would begin to address the critical dimensions of the ecological challenge in a substantive way. Children will undoubtedly have gained a general familiarity with certain aspects of the environmental impasse by this time, and some attention may even have been devoted to a review of specific environmental problems in the early years of the child's education; but were a survey of the critical dimensions of the ecological crisis to be the sole or even primary focus of education in early and middle childhood, the primary tasks of childhood discussed in this and previous chapters—to build an initial relationship to the world and articulate a functional cosmology of the universe—would pass largely unnoticed and unaddressed from an ecological perspective. Thus the "cultural work" of early and middle childhood, while seemingly removed from the most violent and critical aspects of the human treatment of the natural world, actually provides the foundations for moving into a new critical mode of relatedness in adolescence that addresses the underlying dimensions of the ecological challenge.

At the close of Chapter 4 it was noted that the completion of middle childhood is marked in part by the child's need to nourish an independent line of thought and make an initial stand in the world on one's own terms. The transition to adolescence is signaled by a growing sense of discontinuity between the strivings of self, caregivers, and the world at large, and a corresponding existential awakening to the darker (violent) forces at work in the universe. (Of course, this transition manifests itself as a subtle process that gradually unfolds over time in tandem with other psychological and physical changes accompanying puberty.) Inherent to such a transition may be the adolescent's loss of implicit security in the world around her, which signals a shift away from the reciprocal nature of the child/world relationship that characterized middle childhood. An ecologically sensitive approach to education during adolescence would reflect this shift by situating education within an inquiry-based and critical context that can potentially facilitate the acquisition of specific ecologically sensitive understandings, skills, and values:

> In the kind of world that can be easily foreseen . . . [a] cluster of skills must also be considered basic. These are generally characterized as critical thinking skills . . . They are skills which develop in the learner, a keen sense of values of both the natural and intellectual worlds. They involve skills in moral and ethical assessment, projection of implications of alternative world views and decisions for both individuals and community, and the development of ethical principles. (Gillies, 1989, p. 19)

What kinds of ideas are appropriately introduced to adolescents within an ecologically sensitive approach to education? We might begin by bringing into the foreground specific understandings and values that have been implicitly fostered throughout middle childhood—basic notions related to human interdependency with the natural world, ecological and life processes, and a deeply felt respect for the integrity of the wider earth community. We can then help young people to apply these understandings and values to the contemporary ecological and social problems faced by communities around the world. In recognizing the multifaceted nature of the environmental challenge, we can explore with students the ecological, economic, cultural, and other dimensions of the ecological challenge, assess the global and local repercussions of rapid environmental change, and build connections with other social issues, including peace and social justice challenges, human rights and development issues, and concerns over poverty and violence. Concurrently, the ability to pose problems and frame questions in terms of the wider cultural and ecological implications of human actions and motives needs to be reinforced. The ecologically problematic aspects of modernism, including deeply entrenched notions such as "freedom," "individualism," and "progress," need to be critiqued in terms of their contributions to the cultural dimensions of the ecological challenge. Ecologically sensitive practices, including agricultural, technological, and economic ones that extend from both Western and non-Western traditions, need to be studied, and the cultural beliefs which underlie these practices explored. Finally, we need to support young people as they struggle to formulate and articulate the basic foundations of a new vision for the future, one that is ecologically sustainable, culturally feasible, and celebrational in its vision of the reengagement of the human to the natural world. We need to help young people to develop the necessary critical, practical, lifestyle, and social action skills they will need in order to bring this vision into reality.

The above understandings can be reinforced in adolescence partly through a wide-ranging exploration of the core motifs of human and earth history. In many ways, education in adolescence can continue to proceed within a narrative context, not unlike that invoked during middle childhood. However, whereas the majesty and reciprocity of the early formative forces of earth history emerged as the essential points of reference for younger children, the more critical dimensions of this story are more properly introduced in adolescence. Earlier in this chapter the story of the universe was traced [in reference to Swimme and Berry (1992)] up to the rise of the first human communities during the Neolithic period of earth history. The emergence of the great classical civilizations and the period of modern history which follows the Neolithic age presents adolescents with an appropriate historical context for learning about many of the social, political, philosophical, scientific, and technological achievements of the modern period. Likewise, framed within an ecological context, such an account provides a suitable launching point for addressing the antecedent roots of contemporary ecological, economic, and cultural challenges:

> Five thousand years ago, as human urbanization intensified, modest villages gave way to the great urban centers of classical civilizations: Babylon, Paris, Rome, Jerusalem, Constantinople, Athens, Cairo, Mecca, and Delhi, etc. New social arrangements based on hierarchical forms of authority and economic specialization arose in these cities to organize the massive populations into productive units. The natural landscapes of the populated regions of the world came to be marked in their human presence by cultural and technological achievements in architecture, irrigation, mining, and other domains. With commercial endeavors flourishing and population growth on the rise, wealth gradually came to be concentrated in the hands of the few — the great Kings and Pharaohs of this period. The powerful directed massive military and economic campaigns which traversed the planet in an effort to win greater territory and reap nature's bounty. At home, city centers fortified themselves in an effort to protect their wealth as rivalrous military campaigns were waged against them. Throughout this period,

the notion of the divine Spirit, that Neolithic spiritual symbol of human engagement with the wider earth community, was unceremoniously recast as a set of warring deities.

Turbulent as these centuries were, this period also saw the emergence of philosophy as a reflective practice, the invention of writing, and the rise of the great religious traditions, including Christianity, Buddhism, and Islam. The emergence of philosophy signaled a human readiness to ponder the human condition and human sociality at an analytical level of consciousness. With the invention of writing there emerged the ability to maintain historical records, to inscribe moral and religious codes of authority, and to transfer these and other writings intact from generation to generation. In Europe, the Middle East, India, and China, the great religions came to pervade each of the world's great city centers. Only sub-Saharan Africa, the great civilizations of the Americas (e.g., the Mayan and Inca cultures), and a minority of Aboriginal communities scattered around the world remained unaffected by these powerful cultural forces.

Just over 500 years ago, in an effort to colonize the civilizations of the world and build lasting trade relations with the Far East, European endeavors in the Americas, Australia, India, and elsewhere marked the beginning of the move toward political and economic globalization throughout the world. Concurrently, the notion of the nation-state as the primary unit of community life came to dominate international relations in Europe. The basic tenets of mechanistic science (critiqued here in Chapter 1) came to pervade scientific inquiry in the West. Political ideology, the legal and property rights of individuals vs. the social collective, the bureaucratic organization of the state, and near religious incarnations of nationalist pride came to dominate the political and economic process and prompted the rise of two new forms of social organization—liberal democracy and social communism. Tensions within and between states, particularly related to notions of freedom and democracy, marked the great revolutions of this period [i.e., the American Revolution (1776), the French Revolution (1789), and the Russian Revolution (1917)] and the World Wars of the first half of the twentieth century.

Agreement on the core motifs of the last fifty years is difficult to reach. In general, two basic streams of thought seem to be represented in industrialized nations: first, a rosy optimism for the future, based largely on a glorification of the technological marvels of the modern age and the promise of increased prosperity to follow; second, widespread disillusionment within marginalized groups, the poor, and minorities over the failings of liberal democracy to equalize access to economic and social resources. Despite the contradictions between these two vantage points, there does seem to be one overriding social condition which pervades both. The end of World War II signaled our entry into the nuclear era, an age marked by a dawning awareness of the human power to shape its destiny and that of the wider earth community on a scale never before seen. In the years since World War II, the sheer rapidity of technological innovation has come to dominate the lives of the world's most privileged citizens and resulted in the stepped-up plundering of the earth's resources. However, only now are the cultural and ecological implications of such "advancements" beginning to be fully understood. This situation is exacerbated by the move toward increased globalization on the economic and political fronts that has unleashed economic forces no single nation can hope to manage independently. The move toward economic globalization is epitomized by the debt crises currently faced by many industrialized and developing nations and by the rise of the multinational corporation, huge conglomerates which hold vast amounts of economic and political power and control a large proportion of the earth's resources and the world's labor.

As we move from an exploration of the central themes and legacies of the modern period to a consideration of the future, education in adolescence might well be framed around a series of pressing questions that will likely need to be resolved in the coming years—one way or another—by today's generation of young people. First, what will be the relationship of the human to the natural world in the coming decades? Can we afford to continue to pull away from nature, to see the natural world merely as a resource for human use and exploitation, or is a new era of human reengagement to the natural world upon us? Second, how should the essential quality of our relationship to the wider earth community be defined? Are there basic moral principles we can articulate that can guide us in our dealings with the natural world? How should our human institutions and professions—political, economic, religious, scientific, legal, medical, educational, and others—be redefined in light of the ecological challenge? Finally, how do we reconcile the social, political, and technological achievements of the modern period with the problematic role some of these have played in contributing to the ecological problems we face? Are certain achievements of the modern period, such as the unique worth our legal and political institutions now assign to the individual, worth preserving? If so, how can these achievements be made congruent with the needs of a threatened earth community? Supporting young people as they struggle to deal with these and many other fundamental questions needs to be judged from the present moment onward as a primary indicator of quality instruction within an ecologically sensitive approach to education.

THE RECOVERY OF THE IDEA AND THE ROLE
OF THE CHILD IN SOCIETY

This book has argued that children are uniquely positioned to play an integral role in changing the course of human and earth history. Children's plasticity of response to change, aptitude for wonder, natural inquisitiveness, and need to frame an initial relationship to the world could together serve as a pivotal point of intervention for helping the next generation to build an ecologically sensitive relationship to the world. By playing a caring role in the lives of children and in recognizing childhood as a distinct ontological stage within the human life span, with possibilities and constraints set apart from those of adulthood, caregivers can provide children with the support they need in order to co-construct an ecologically sensitive cosmology of the world. This chapter has argued that an elementary curriculum which emphasizes the study of *place, form, story*, and *earth literacy* can support children's search for meaning and purpose in the world and help them to build a functional cosmology of the universe.

It is a celebration of reciprocity between the cultural life of humans and the functioning of the natural world, and a recognition of the integral role that children can play in the recovery of the earth process, which is at the heart of such an ecological vision of childhood and education. But such a vision needs to be supported by an equally compelling role for children in society at present, an opportunity for children to participate as something more than, for example, a captive audience for advertisers, television networks, and video game manufacturers.

As teachers, parents, and caregivers, we need to involve children in ecologically and culturally significant endeavors that restore natural places and richly textured play and learning spaces to cities and strengthen ties to local communities. To sustain these initiatives, we need to renew our commitment to make our cities safe for men, women, and children alike. The importance of children's participation in religious ceremonies and community festivals that celebrate the earth community needs to be recognized, as does the importance of providing children with culturally significant rites of passage into adolescence and adulthood. We need to bring children and the elderly back into the mainstream of the cultural life of our communities and nurture culturally significant relationships between young and old. We need to support children as they endeavor to construct a narrative account of their lives and build a "working theory" of the natural, physical, cultural, and moral worlds that surround them. The choices we make as teachers, parents, caregivers, and citizens in forging an ecologically significant role for children needs to be seen as one of the most important cultural indicators that we have at present in evaluating the future viability of our species and the wider earth community.

At the beginning of Chapter 1, it was argued that we presently face a critical turning point in our relationship to the balance of life on the planet. How we respond to the ecological challenge in the coming decades—for example, whether we choose a Technozoic or an Ecozoic future—will largely determine our long-term viability as a species and the future health of the earth community. While it is true that effective change will be brought about only through conscious decision making and decisive action on the part of governments and industry in the macro-level political and economic arenas, it is also true that there is much "cultural work" to be done at the level of the individual, the family, and the community. This book has argued that educators, in their unique position as intergenerational cultural intermediaries—*adults who help children to become at home in the world*—are poised to play an important leadership role in helping children to recover a sense of relationship with the wider earth community. Moving from an anthropocentric view to a biocentric view of the educational process is a laudable first step, but such a move will also need to be grounded within a new biocentric vision of development in childhood in which the role of the child in the recovery of sustainable relations with the natural world is clearly revealed. Articulating such a vision for childhood and education remains one of the most pressing tasks of education. Such a vision establishes the basis for a new story of development in childhood and points to the role of the child in the recovery of the ecological imperative in contemporary society.

Ecologically Sensitive Change in Schools

Educators today are inundated with numerous strategies for educational change in schools. These strategies run the gamut from top-down ministry-mandated reforms to grass roots community initiatives. The more holistic of these reform initiatives stress the importance of collegiality and collaboration throughout the change process. Most do not, however, directly address the needs of the global environment. In this respect, something more is called for within the change process, for no strategy, holistic or otherwise, can ensure that an environmentally sensitive approach to change in schools is adopted unless this is the clear intention of all stakeholders from the outset of the reform process. Regardless of the effectiveness of change strategies, educational reform efforts can nevertheless end up being "juxtaposed to," rather than "congruent with," the needs of the local ecosystem, bioregion, and wider earth community.

An ecologically sensitive view of educational reform is marked by the move from an anthropocentric to a biocentric theory of change. At the level of *infrastructure*, the environmental impact of changes to the day-to-day operations of schools—for example, in the usage of resources and in the physical structure of the school (and surrounding neighborhood)—need to be addressed. At an *ideological* level, curricular reforms and subject matter that subtly advance an exploitive and utilitarian view of the natural world need to be challenged. There are also *methodological* issues at stake here. For example, reforms that lead to the further fragmentation and compartmentalization of school curricula are inherently hostile to the ecological approaches to thinking that need to be nurtured in schools. Addressing each of these areas—infrastructure, ideology, and methodology—is integral to the development of a sustainable theory of change in schools.

Although the previous chapters have focused primarily on the curricu-

155

lar foundations of an ecologically sensitive approach to education, ecologically sensitive change in schools can also be initiated on a variety of complementary levels—from the basic structural foundations of schools (e.g., concerns over material usage and waste disposal) to the relatively painless reforms of incorporating environmentally sensitive statements into board-level documents, teacher's union literature, and school conduct codes. Although important in themselves, each of these efforts ultimately rests within the context of a much larger environmental reform movement which is just now beginning to address the important role of schools in securing a sustainable future world for adults, children, and the wider earth community. Our task for the immediate future must be to continue to articulate such a vision for education and build a curricular framework for schools that can best help us recover an authentic human mode of relatedness to the natural world and squarely face up to the ecological challenges which now confront us.

Notes

Chapter 1

1. It is conceivable that an industrial market economy might not have quite so devastating an impact on the planet, if economic growth objectives could be held in check by economic indicators that are sensitive to the ecospheric conditions of the natural world. Yet this has not been the case. Gross national product (GNP), the economist's primary indicator of economic growth, has come under considerable fire because of its exclusive focus on productivity (i.e., *quantity* of economic activity) and complete lack of attention to the effects of that productivity on the environment (i.e., on the *quality* of natural resources). In this sense, doing something— indeed, anything, so long as it is economically productive—is valued regardless of its effect on the natural world. To the degree that one outcome of environmental degradation is the creation of new markets for "clean-up" jobs and technologies, etc., the destruction of the planet can actually contribute to an increase in GNP, as in the case of the 1989 oil spill disaster off the coast of Alaska, in which the costs of clean-up efforts raised the GNP and hence "contributed" to the economic growth of the United States (MacNeill et al., 1991; Gordon and Suzuki, 1990).

2. Herman Daly (1989) comments further on the conceptual problems associated with a circular view of economic flow (i.e., Figure 1.1):

> Economists are interested in scarcity, and during the formative years of economic theory the environment was considered, with some reason, an infinite source of raw materials and an infinite sink for waste materials, so the throughput was not scarce and was naturally abstracted from. Only scarce items entered into exchange, and exchange value flowed in a circle. So the circular flow became the paradigm within which we sought to understand the economic process. Once the throughput itself became scarce then the circular flow vision became economically, as well as physically, misleading. It totally obscured the emerging scarcity of environmental services. The circular flow has no beginning and no end, no points of contact with anything outside itself. Therefore it cannot possibly register the costs of depletion and pollution, nor the irreversible historical effects induced by the entropic nature of the throughput. (p. 76)

The flow diagram is a closed system which measures the *quantity* of economic activity through the system (throughput), but it is alienated from the wider effects of that activity on the declining *quality* of natural resource stocks and ecospheric processes. Citing the entropy law of thermodynamics, Daly (1991) argues that the cycling of energy (and recycling of natural resources) through the production process necessarily implies a gradual depreciation in the quality of those resources through "friction, rust, accident, loss, decay, and so on" (p. 146) as the once richly concentrated minerals are broken down and dispersed.

Chapter 2

1. Daly (1989, p. 75) writes that "much confusion could be avoided if we could agree to use the word 'growth' to refer only to the quantitative scale of the physical dimensions of the economy. Qualitative improvement could be labeled 'development.' Then we could speak of a steady-state economy as one which develops without growing, just as the planet Earth, of which the economy is an open subsystem, develops without growing. Growth of the economic organism means larger jaws and a bigger digestive tract. Development means more complete digestion and wiser purposes. Limits to growth do not imply limits to development."

2. Although it is true that some representatives of big business are strong advocates of compensatory and nutrition programs for poor children, their support for these programs is rarely founded on feelings of solidarity with disadvantaged children per se; rather their rationale for such programs is based on the likelihood that healthy and well-nourished children will be better able to contribute to economic development in the long run and less likely to be a burden on the public purse. From this perspective, social programs are valued (and funded) only so long as they yield "high rates of return" economically and support the drive for a competitive edge internationally (for example, see Kearns and Doyle, 1988, p. 113). If, for some reason, the contributions of compensatory and nutritional programs to economic growth should become less certain, it is likely that these social programs would be roundly criticized by technocratic proponents for being misguided and economically wasteful.

3. In their appraisal of the failings of the free school movement, Aronowitz and Giroux (1993, p. 19) write that "radical school reform of the 1960s adopted an anti-intellectual stance that helped prepare the victory of the right. They surrendered the concept of systematic knowledge acquisition and uncritically privileged an anti-intellectual concept of student experience. This ideology constituted merely the mirror image of the cognitive orientation of school officials which prescribed a set of learnings prior to any possible experience. Thus the radical reformers were prey to the charge that they had betrayed the interests of the poor and minorities, who desperately needed to learn how to read, write, and calculate."

4. It is interesting (and perhaps significant) that an opportunity for solitude and quiet contemplation generally appears not to have been provided for students, even in those progressive schools which professed to hold an extreme child-centered ideology. Although Dewey himself recognized the importance of allowing children "brief intervals of time for quiet reflection" (1938/1963, p. 63), his more popularized view of cognitive development equated learning with purposeful activity, which perhaps explains (in part) why an *intense* level of activity (and commotion?) has

been judged by some progressive educators to be a primary characteristic of the successful child-centered classroom. Nearly forty years later, John Holt (1969) wrote that one major criticism of the British progressive (primary) schools was that children were expected to be constantly busy. These schools equated long periods of sustained activity with success in learning, and in Holt's view, did not allow children to have sufficient time alone or opportunity for private reflection (see similar criticisms in Sharp and Green, 1975). Thus the children (who had to satisfy their teachers that they were constantly busy) were prevented from engaging in specific acts of contemplation, individualized periods of "incubation of thought" that (perhaps) originated in perplexity but culminated in the illumination of an idea. Contrast this with the holistic attitude toward contemplative practices discussed by John P. Miller (1988).

5. Recent efforts by some global educators to link a holistic conception of education to peace and social justice issues could provide holistic educators with an important context for linking the holistic philosophy to a number of important political and cultural struggles. For example, see the work of Sue Greig, David Selby, and Graham Pike (1987).

Chapter 3

1. There are some exceptions to the contrasts drawn here between progressive and holistic conceptions of childhood. For example, there are certain parallels between the progressive conception of the child and the Montessori tradition in holistic education.

2. Were an apprenticeship-style approach to education to have continued into the modern age, many of the environmental problems we now face may never have occurred. As the Smith quotation [and the Pulliam (1987) quotation from Chapter 2] clearly indicate, institutionalized mass schooling originally developed within the same mechanistic mindset that underlay the human domination of the natural world throughout the industrial era. Therefore it is conceivable that the absence of such a mindset would not only have lessened our impact on the environment, but also precluded the development of a formalized system of education.

Chapter 4

1. It is appropriate that this statement should refer only to males. The theories of child development advanced by both Rousseau and Froebel (discussed later in the chapter) took account of only male experience and either ignored the female child (in the case of Froebel) or relegated female experience to the point of contempt (in the case of Rousseau). In the discussion below, I have taken the liberty of partially "degenderizing" passages taken from Froebel's writing, but it should be kept in mind that his conception of childhood was developed exclusively from a male vantage point. Although it is not addressed within the scope of the present book, the need to account for gender differences in ecologically sensitive theories of child development emerges as an important theme for further inquiry.

2. For a detailed comparison of the Montessori and Froebel theories of education, see Chapter 19 of E. M. Standing (1957/1984).

3. In recent years, a study by Louise Chawla (1986) has called into question the universality of the peak experiences reported by Cobb's subjects. In a review of the autobiographical experiences of 38 creative thinkers and entrepreneurs—artists, businesspeople, scientists, and politicians—Chawla found that in general only subjects who were artists by vocation reported having had momentary experiences of intense identification with the natural world during childhood. In sharp contrast, a number of scientists reported a sense of detachment from the environment in childhood—an orientation that perhaps foreshadowed the objectivity that would later be required of them in their careers. For other respondents, it was neither the quality of a childhood environment nor growing up in a "rural" or an "urban" setting which held the most significance in terms of the development of self; rather it was the sense of security and reassurance afforded by a particular environment, "a sense of belonging to a place, a sense of knowing that this place is where one belongs" (p. 40). Compare this finding with the discussion in Chapter 5 that explores the impact of community violence on children living in danger.

Chapter 5

1. When the true intentions of arguments advocating the use of violence against children are revealed, we are likely to find many commonalities, such as: (1) an appeal to tradition, a greater authority, or otherworldly forces to substantiate the use of violence against children; (2) validation for parents who engage in violent action against their children and scorn for parents who do not; (3) the use of the fear factor and predictions of adolescent delinquency if physical punishment is withheld; (4) a disassociation of the element of violence from the violent act, which is then seen to be an expression of the parent's love for the child; (5) a sanctioning of violence as a last resort; and (6) a masking of any of the above within a seemingly well-intentioned or otherwise persuasive argument.

2. The notion of a "protected period" of development during early and middle childhood raises the important question of whether or not children's sense of security might unintentionally be jeopardized by educators' attempts to address the most violent aspects of environmental and other crises. As will be argued at the close of Chapter 6, a focus on the most violent aspects of the environmental crisis is perhaps congruent with the developmental tasks of adolescence, but it largely works against the primary developmental tasks of early and middle childhood, namely, to build an initial relationship to the world and articulate a functional cosmology of the universe.

Chapter 6

1. The curvature of space principle also has application beyond the natural world. At a cultural level, it can account for many of our aesthetic notions of beauty as reflected in architecture, mathematics, and music, etc. It can account for important debates within social philosophy. Ideological tensions between the rights

of individuals (differentiation) versus the social collective (integration) in moral, political, and legal philosophy can be directly related to the curvature of space principle, for example. Perhaps most significantly, given the subject matter of this book, this principle can also be applied to specific conceptions of development in childhood, including Paul Shepard's view of development as "resonating between disjunction and unity" (1982, p. 109) and my own model of childhood (see Figure 4.1 in Chapter 4), which represents middle childhood as being nearly perfectly balanced between the early childhood and adolescent forces of differentiation (mastery) and integration (immersion). Also see Robert Kegan (1982) for a developmental view that similarly parallels the curvature of space principle.

References

Altman, I., & Chemers, M. (1980). *Culture and environment.* Monterey, CA: Brooks/Cole.

Aries, P. (1962). *Centuries of childhood: A social history of family life.* New York: Vintage Books.

Armstrong, T. (1984). Transpersonal experience in childhood. *Journal of Transpersonal Psychology, 16*(2), 207–230.

Armstrong, T. (1985). *The radiant child.* Wheaton, IL: The Theosophical Publishing House.

Aronowitz, S., & Giroux, H. A. (1993). *Education still under siege.* Toronto: OISE Press.

Atwell, N. (1987). *In the middle: Writing, reading, and learning with adolescents.* Portsmouth, NH: Heinemann Publishers.

Bailey, T. (1991). Jobs of the future and the education they will require: Evidence from occupational forecasts. *Educational Researcher, 20*(2), 11–20.

Baker, C. D., & Freebody, P. (1989). *Children's first school books.* Oxford: Basil Blackwell.

Berger, J. (1979). *Pig earth.* New York: Pantheon Books.

Berry, T. (1988). *The dream of the earth.* San Francisco: Sierra Club Books.

Berry, T. (1989). Coming of age in the ecozoic era. *Katuah Journal, 26,* 1–3.

Bishop, J. H., & Carter, S. (1991). How accurate are recent BLS occupational projections? *Monthly Labor Review, 114*(10), 37–43.

Bohm, D. (1983). *Wholeness and the implicate order.* London: Ark.

Bowers, C. A. (1993). *Education, cultural myths, and the ecological crisis: Toward deep changes.* Albany: SUNY Press.

Breiner, S. J. (1990). *Slaughter of the innocents: Child abuse through the ages and today.* New York: Plenum Press.

Bronfenbrenner, U. (1979). *The ecology of human development: Experiments by nature and design.* Cambridge: Harvard University Press.

Brown, L. (Ed.). (1986). *State of the World, 1986.* New York: W. W. Norton.

Brumberg, J. (1988). *Fasting girls: The emergence of anorexia as a modern disease.* Cambridge: Harvard University Press.

Caduto, M. J., & Bruchac, J. (1989). *Keepers of the earth.* Saskatoon: Fifth House Publishers.

Canfield, J., & Wells, H. C. (1976). *100 ways to enhance self-concept in the classroom.* Englewoods Cliffs, NJ: Prentice-Hall.

Capra, F. (1975). *The tao of physics.* New York: Shambhala.

Carlgren, F. (1976). *Education towards freedom: A survey of the work of Waldorf schools throughout the world.* East Grinstead, UK: Lanthorn Press.

Carnoy, M. (1987). High technology and education: An economist's view. In K. Benne & S. Tozer (Eds.), *Society as educator in an age of transition* (pp. 88–111). Chicago: University of Chicago Press.

Carson, R. (1956/1990). *The sense of wonder.* Berkeley: The Nature Company.

Chawla, L. (1986). The ecology of environmental memory. *Children's Environment Quarterly, 3*(4), 34–42.

Clark, E. T. (1991). Holism: Implications of the new paradigm. *Holistic Education Review, 4*(2), 43–48.

Cobb, E. (1969). The ecology of imagination in childhood. In D. McKinley & P. Shepard (Eds.), *The subversive science: Essays toward an ecology of man* (pp. 122–132). Boston: Houghton Mifflin.

Cobb, E. (1977). *The ecology of imagination in childhood.* New York: Columbia University Press.

Cohen, B. L. (1984). Statement of dissent. In J. L. Simon & H. Kahn (Eds.), *The resourceful earth: A response to Global 2000* (p. 566). New York: Basil Blackwell.

Cohn, D., et al. (1990). Parallel paths: A conversation among Montessori and Waldorf educators. *Holistic Education Review, 3*(4), 40–50.

Coles, R. (1986). *The moral life of children.* Boston: Atantic Monthly Press.

Collins, W. A. (1984). The status of basic research on middle childhood. In W. A. Collins (Ed.), *Development during middle childhood: The years from six to twelve* (pp. 390–421). Washington, DC: National Academy Press.

Committee for Economic Development. (1985). *Investing in our future: Business and the public schools.* New York: Research and Policy Committee Division.

Common, M. (1988). *Environmental and resource economics: An introduction.* London: Longman Group.

Counts, G. S. (1932/1969). *Dare the school build a new social order?* New York: Arno Press.

Cremin, L. (1982). *The transformation of the school: Progressivism in American education, 1876–1957.* New York: Alfred A. Knopf.

Cropper, M. L., & Oates, W. E. (1992). Environmental economics: A survey. *Journal of Economic Literature, 30*, 675–740.

Curtis, S. J., & Boultwood, M. (1956). *A short history of educational ideas.* London: University Tutorial Press.

Daly, H. E. (1989). Steady-state and growth concepts for the next generation. In F. Archibugi & P. Nijkamp (Eds.), *Economy and ecology: Towards sustainable development* (pp. 73–87). Dordrecht, The Netherlands: Kluwer Academic Publishers.

Daly, H. (1991). The steady-state economy. In A. Dobson (Ed.), *The green reader* (pp. 145–151). London: Andre Deutsch Limited.

Davy, J. (1973, March 23). The movement that everyone tries to forget. *The Times.*

de Mause, L. (1988). The evolution of childhood. In L. de Mause (Ed.), *The history of childhood: The untold story of child abuse* (pp. 1–73). New York: Peter Bedrick Books.

Dewey, J. (1916/1966). *Democracy and education*. New York: The Free Press.

Dewey, J. (1938/1963). *Experience and education*. New York: Macmillan.

DeYoung, A. J. (1989). *Economics and American education: A historical and critical overview of the impact of economic theories on schooling in the United States*. New York: Longman.

Dineen, J. (1992, Nov. 2). A tree grows in Toronto. The *Toronto Star*, pp. B1–B3.

Dixon, R. G. D. (1992). *Future schools*. Toronto: ECW Press.

Durning, A. (1991). Asking how much is enough. In L. R. Brown (Ed.), *State of the World, 1991* (pp. 153–169). New York: W. W. Norton.

Economic Council of Canada. (1992). *A lot to learn: Education and training in Canada*. Ottawa: Ministry of Supply and Services.

Ehrlich, P. (1991). *Healing the planet: Strategies for resolving the environmental crisis*. Reading, MA: Addison Wesley.

Ehrlich, P., et al. (1973). *Human ecology: Problems and solutions*. San Francisco: W. H. Freeman.

Evergreen Foundation. (1994). *A guide to school ground naturalization: Welcoming back the wilderness*. Toronto: Prentice-Hall.

Farson, R. (1974). *Birthrights*. New York: Penguin Books.

Food Works. (1992). *The Common Roots Program*. Montpelier, VT: Foodworks.

Fowler, J. W. (1981). *Stages of faith: The psychology of human development and the quest for meaning*. San Francisco: Harper & Row Publishers.

Freeman, M. (1991). *Before I am, we are*. Unpublished paper, Queen's Unversity, Kingston, Canada.

Freud, S. (1896). *The aetiology of hysteria*. Vienna: Vienna Society for Psychiatry and Neurology.

Froebel, F. (1826/1912). *Froebel's chief writings on education*. New York: Longman.

Garbarino, J., et al. (1992). *Children in danger: Coping with the consequences of community violence*. San Francisco: Jossey-Bass.

Gardner, H. (1991). *The unschooled mind: How children think and how schools should teach*. San Francisco: HarperCollins.

Gelb, S. (1991). Not necessarily the new paradigm: Holism and the future. *Holistic Education Review, 4*(2), 37–42.

Gillies, H. E. (1989). *Post-industrial futures papers*. Toronto: Post-industrial Futures Companies and Government Organizations.

Gilligan, C. (1985). *Two moral orientations: Implications for thinking about moral development and moral education of women and men*. Toronto: Controversial Issues in Moral Education Conference.

Gordon, A., & Suzuki, D. (1990). *It's a matter of survival*. Toronto: Stoddart Publishing.

Greig, S., Selby, D., & Pike, G. (1987). *Earthrights: Education as if the planet really mattered*. London: The World Wildlife Fund.

Greig, S., Selby, D., & Pike, G. (1989). *Greenprints for changing schools*. London: World Wildlife Fund/Kegan Page.

Greven, P. (1991). *Spare the child: The religious roots of punishment and psychological impact of physical abuse*. New York: Alfred A. Knopf.

Gutek, G. L. (1974). *Philosophical alternatives in education*. Columbus, OH: Charles E. Merrill.

Hadlock, P., Hecker, D., & Gannon, J. (1991). High technology employment: Another view. *Monthly Labor Review, 114*(7), 26–30.

Harste, J. C., & Short, K. (1988). *Creating classrooms for authors: The reading-writing connection*. Portsmouth, NH: Heinemann.

Hart, R. (1979). *Children's experience of place*. New York: Irvington.

Harwood, A. C. (1958). *The recovery of man in childhood*. London: Hodder and Stoughton.

Holt, J. (1969). *How children learn*. New York: Pitman Publishing.

Homer-Dixon, T. F., Boutwell, J. H., & Rathjens, G. W. (1993). Environmental change and violent conflict. *Scientific American, 268*(2), 38–45.

Hunt, F. J. (1988). *The incorporation of education: An international study of the transformation of educational priorities*. London: Routledge & Kegan Paul.

Hutchison, D. (1991). The spiritual realm within a holistic conception of child development and education. *Holistic Education Review, 4*(3), 12–22.

James, A., & Prout, A. (1990). Introduction. In A. James & A. Prout (Eds.), *Constructing and reconstructing childhood: Contemporary issues in the sociological study of childhood* (pp. 1–6). London: Falmer Press.

Johnson, A. (1991). Whole thinking and the process of human development. *Holistic Education Review, 4*(2), 17–22.

Kahn, D. (1980). *A parent's guide to Montessori elementary*. Cleveland: North American Montessori Teachers' Association.

Kahn, D. (1991). The Montessori contribution to educational reform. *North American Montessori Teachers' Association Journal, 16*(2), 1–12.

Karier, C. J. (1986). *The individual, society, and education: A history of American educational ideas* (2nd ed.). Chicago: University of Illinois Press.

Kearns, D. T., & Doyle, D. P. (1988). *Winning the brain race: A bold plan to make our schools competitive*. San Francisco: Institute for Contemporary Studies Press.

Kegan, R. (1982). *The evolving self: Problem and process in human development*. Cambridge: Harvard University Press.

Kessen, W. (1983). The child and other cultural inventions. In F. Kessel & A. W. Siegel (Eds.), *The child and other cultural inventions* (pp. 26–39). New York: Praeger.

Kilpatrick, W. H. (1927). *Education for a changing civilization*. New York: Macmillan.

Kluckhohn, F. R. (1953). Dominant and variant value orientations. In C. Kluckhohn & H. A. Murray (Eds.), *Personality in nature, society, and culture* (pp. 342–357). New York: Knopf.

Kohlberg, L., & Mayer, R. (1978). Development as the aim of education. In J. Gress & D. Purpel (Eds.), *Curriculum*. Berkeley: McCutchan.

Konner, M. (1991). *Childhood*. Boston: Little, Brown.

Krauthammer, C. (1990, Feb. 5). Education: Doing bad and feeling good. *Time*, p. 64.

La Haye, B. (1977). *How to develop your child's temperament*. Eugene, OR: Harvest House Publishers.

Lilley, I. M. (1967). *Friedrich Froebel*. London: Cambridge University Press.

Link-Brenkman, J. (1983). Seeing beyond the interests of industry: Teaching critical thinking. *Journal of Education, 165*(3), 283–294.

Lockhart, A. (1977). Educational policy development in Canada: A critique of the past and a case for the future. In R. Carlton (Ed.), *Education, change, and society* (pp. 77–88). Toronto: Gage.

Loughmiller, C. (1965). *Wilderness road*. Texas: Hogg Foundation for Mental Health.

Loughmiller, C. (1974). *Kids in trouble*. Texas: Wildwood Books.

MacNeill, J., et al. (1991). *Beyond interdependence: The meshing of the world's economy and the earth's ecology*. New York: Oxford University Press.

Masson, J. M. (1984). *The assault on truth: Freud's suppression of the seducation theory*. Toronto: Collins Publishers.

Matthews, G. B. (1980). *Philosophy and the young child*. Cambridge: Harvard University Press.

McMurtry, J. (1989, December 28). Education for sale, from Harvard to Hong Kong. *The Toronto Star*, p. A19.

Mead, M. (1978). *Culture and commitment*. Garden City, NY: Anchor.

Michelet, J. (1846/1973). *The people*. Urbana, IL: University of Illinois Press.

Miller, A. (1984a). *For your own good: Hidden cruelty in child-rearing and the roots of violence*. Toronto: Collins Publishers.

Miller, A. (1984b). *Thou shalt not be aware: Society's betrayal of the child*. New York: Farrar Straus Giroux.

Miller, A. (1990). *Banished knowledge: Facing childhood injuries*. New York: Doubleday.

Miller, J. P. (1988). *The holistic curriculum*. Toronto: OISE Press.

Miller, J. P., & Seller, W. (1985). *Curriculum: Perspectives and practice*. New York: Longman.

Miller, J. P., Cassie, J. R., & Drake, S. M. (1990). *Holistic learning: A teacher's guide to integrated studies*. Toronto: OISE Press.

Miller, R. (1990). *What are schools for? Holistic education in American culture*. Brandon, VT: Holistic Education Press.

Miller, R. (1991a). Editorial: Passing the torch. *Holistic Education Review, 4*(4), 2–3.

Miller, R. (1991b). Some reflections on this discussion. *Holistic Education Review, 4*(2), 49–50.

Miller, R. (1992). Defining a common vision: The holistic movement in the U.S. *Orbit, 23*(2), 20–21.

Montessori, M. (1948/1967). *To educate the human potential*. Adyar, Madras, India: Kalakshetra Publications.

Montessori, M. (1948/1973). *From childhood to adolescence*. New York: Schocken Books.

Moore, R. C. (1986). *Childhood's domain: Play and place in child development*. London: Croom Helm.

Nabhan, G. P., & Trimble, S. (1994). *The geography of childhood: Why children need wild places*. Boston: Beacon Press.

National Center for Children in Poverty. (1990). *Five million children: A statistical profile of our poorest young citizens*. New York: School of Public Health, Columbia University.

Neatby, H. (1953). *So little for the mind: An indictment of Canadian education*. Toronto: Clarke, Irwin, and Company.

Neill, A. S. (1960). *Summerhill: A radical approach to child rearing*. New York: Hart.

Ontario Ministry of Education. (1985). *Shared discovery: Teaching and learning in the primary years*. Toronto: Ontario Ministry of Education.

Opie, I., & Opie, P. (1959). *The lore and language of schoolchildren*. Oxford: Clarendon Press.

Opie, I., & Opie, P. (1969). *Children's games in street and playground: Chasing, catching, seeking, hunting, racing, duelling, exerting, daring, guessing, acting, pretending*. Oxford: Clarendon Press.

Orr, D. W. (1992). *Ecological literacy: Education and the transition to a postmodern world*. Albany: SUNY Press.

Orteza y Miranda, E. (1982). Pragmatism and the child: John Dewey. In P. T. Rooke & R. L. Schnell (Eds.), *Studies in childhood history: A Canadian perspective* (pp. 29–56). Calgary: Detselig Enterprises Limited.

Pearce, J. C. (1992). *Evolution's end: Claiming the potential of our intelligence*. San Francisco: HarperCollins.

Pelkki, J. A. (1994). The Saginaw River project. *Green Teacher*, (37), 32–33.

Piaget, J. (1929). *The child's conception of the world*. London: Routledge & Kegan Paul.

Piaget, J. (1973). *The child and reality*. New York: Penguin Books.

Polakow, V. (1992). *The erosion of childhood* (2nd ed.). Chicago: University of Chicago Press.

Postel, S., & Flavin, C. (1991). Reshaping the global economy. In L. R. Brown (Ed.), *State of the World, 1991* (pp. 170–188). New York: W. W. Norton & Company.

Postman, N. (1984). "The ascent of humanity": A coherent curriculum. In K. Ryan & J. M. Cooper (Eds.), *Kaleidoscope: Readings in education* (pp. 219–223). Boston: Houghton Mifflin.

Postman, N. (1985). *The disappearance of childhood*. London: Comet Books.

Postman, N. (1995). *The end of education: Redefining the value of school*. New York: Alfred A. Knopf.

Prescott, E. (1987). Environment as organizer of intent in child-care settings. In C. S. Weinstein & T. G. David (Eds.), *Spaces for children: The built environment and child development* (pp. 73–88). New York: Plenum Press.

Pulliam, J. D. (1987). *History of education in America* (4th ed.). Columbus, OH: Merrill Publishing Company.

Purdy, L. M. (1992). *In their best interests?: The case against equal rights for children*. Ithaca, NY: Cornell University Press.

Purpel, D. E. (1989). *The moral and spiritual crisis in education: A curriculum for justice and compassion in education*. Granby, MA: Bergin & Garvey.

Purpel, D. E., & Miller, R. (1991). How whole is holistic education? *Holistic Education Review, 4*(2), 33–36.

Rees, W. (1989). *The ecological meaning of environment-economy integration.* Vancouver: School of Community and Regional Planning, University of British Columbia.

Reich, E. L. (1990). *Economic treads in perspective.* New York: Knopf.

Rickard, H. C., & Latel, K. A. (1974). Group problem-solving in a therapeutic summer camp: An illustration. In H. C. Richard & M. Dinoff (Eds.), *Behaviour modification in children* (pp. 82–95). Tuscaloosa, AL: University of Alabama Press.

Rifkin, J. (1995). *The end of work.* New York: G. P. Putnam's Sons.

Robertson, J. (1983). *The sane alternative: A choice of futures.* Wolverhampton, UK: Gibbons Bavord Print.

Robinson, E. (1977). *The original vision: A study of the religious experience of childhood.* Oxford: Religious Experience Research Unit, Manchester College.

Rousseau, J.-J. (1762/1979). *Émile.* New York: Basic Books.

Scarborough Board of Education. (1988). *Social and Environmental Studies Curriculum, Grade 5.* Scarborough, Ontario: Program Department.

Schneck, M. (1991). *Patterns in nature: A world of color, shape, and light.* New York: Crescent Books.

Seager, J. (1995). *The new state of the earth atlas* (2nd ed.). New York: Simon & Schuster.

Searles, H. F. (1960). *The non-human environment in normal development and in schizophrenia.* New York: International Universities Press, Inc.

Sharp, R., & Green, A. (1975). *Education and social control: A study in progressive primary education.* London: Routledge & Kegan Paul.

Shepard, P. (1967). *Man in the landscape: A historic view of the esthetics of nature.* New York: Alfred A. Knopf.

Shepard, P., & McKinley, D. (Eds.). (1969). *The subversive science: Essays toward an ecology of man.* Boston: Houghton Mifflin.

Shepard, P. (1973). *The tender carnivore and the sacred game.* New York: Charles Scribner's Sons.

Shepard, P. (1977). Place and human development. In *Children, nature, and the urban environment: Proceedings of a symposium-fair* (pp. 7–12). Washington, DC: U.S. Government Printing Office.

Shepard, P. (1982). *Nature and madness.* San Francisco: Sierra Club Books.

Siegler, R. S. (1983). Information processing approaches to development. In P. Mussen (Ed.), *Manual of Child Psychology* (p. 242). New York: John Wiley & Sons.

Simon, J. L. (1981). *The ultimate resource.* Princeton: Princeton University Press.

Smith, G. A. (1992). *Education and the environment: Learning to live with limits.* Albany, NY: SUNY Press.

Sobel, D. (1993). *Children's special places: Exploring the role of forts, dens, and bush houses in middle childhood.* Tucson, AZ: Zephyr Press.

Solzhenitsyn, A., et al. (1974). *From under the rubble.* Boston: Little, Brown.

Standing, E. M. (1957/1984). *Maria Montessori: Her life and work.* New York: Penguin Books.

Steiner, R. (1924/1974). *The kingdom of childhood*. London: Rudolf Steiner Press.

Steiner, R. (1924a/1982). *The roots of education*. London: Rudolf Steiner Press.

Steiner, R. (1924b/1982). *The essentials of education*. London: Rudolf Steiner Press.

Stevens, P. S. (1974). *Patterns in nature*. Boston: Little, Brown.

Stevenson, R. B. (1987). Schooling and environmental education: Contradictions in purpose and practice. In I. Robottom (Ed.), *Environmental education: Practice and possibility* (pp. 69–82). Victoria, Australia: Deakin University Press.

Suzuki, D. (1992, Oct. 17). School "newscasts" pushing consumerism warp values. *The Toronto Star*, p. 7.

Swimme, B., & Berry, T. (1992). *The universe story: From the primordial flaring forth to the Ecozoic era—a celebration of the unfolding of the cosmos*. San Francisco: HarperCollins.

Tanner, J. M. (1978). *Foetus into man: Physical growth from conception to maturity*. Cambridge: Harvard University Press.

Thomas, L. (1983). *Late night thoughts on listening to Mahler's ninth symphony*. New York: Viking Press.

Timberlake, L., & Thomas, L. (1990). *When the bough breaks: Our children, our environment*. London: Earthscan Publications.

UNICEF (1989). *Children and Environment: A UNICEF Strategy for Sustainable Development*. New York: UNICEF.

UNICEF (1993). *State of the World's Children*. New York: UNICEF.

U.S. Department of Energy. (1988). *International Energy Annual*. Washington, DC: U.S. Department of Energy.

Valsiner, J. (1987). *Culture and the development of children's action: A cultural–historical theory of developmental psychology*. Chichester, UK: John Wiley & Sons.

Van Matre, S. (1990). *Earth education: A new beginning*. Warrenville, IL: The Institute for Earth Education.

Vandenberg, D. (1971). *Being and education: An essay in existential phenomenology*. Englewood Cliffs, NJ: Prentice-Hall.

Wartofsky, M. (1983). The child's construction of the world and the world's construction of the child: From historical epistemology to historical psychology. In F. Kessel & A. W. Siegel (Eds.), *The child and other cultural inventions* (pp. 188–223). New York: Praeger Publishers.

Werner, E. E. (1990). Protective factors and individual resilence. In S. J. Meisels & J. P. Shonkoff (Eds.), *Handbook of early childhood intervention* (pp. 97–116). Cambridge: Cambridge University Press.

Whitman, W. (1961). *Collected Writings*. New York: New York University Press.

Zelizer, V. A. (1985). *Pricing the priceless child: The changing economic value of children*. New York: Basic Books.

Index

About the Author

David Hutchison (M.E.S., B.Ed.) is a part-time instructor in the undergraduate teacher education program at the Ontario Institute for Studies in Education and a 1991 recipient of the William Pakenham Fellowship from the Faculty of Education, University of Toronto.